Praise for William Westney's
The Perfect Wrong Note

"Wonderfully frank . . . refreshing . . . a valid resource for anyone playing any instrument."

—*Music Educators Journal*

"An absolute joy to read, with much . . . that stimulates and engages. . . . Westney is asking new questions not addressed elsewhere. . . . You won't fail to be drawn in by the author's inviting yet quietly compelling style."

—*Piano Professional* (U.K.)

"Instructive and controversial. . . . Musicians need to think and re-think what they have been doing and how they have been doing it. Westney's book is a refreshing, amusing and highly informative addition to the debate."

—*Pianist* magazine (U.K.)

"This is a book to be read slowly and studied, not because it is complicated to read, but because it has so many thought-provoking parallels in other facets of life. . . . This book deserves, no demands, a wide readership. . . . The title alone—*The Perfect Wrong Note*—is a stroke of genius."

—*The Lubbock Avalanche-Journal*

"Pianist-educator William Westney asks us to rethink our whole attitude toward mistakes in his book, *The Perfect Wrong Note*, suggesting that clunkers have value after all."

—*Los Angeles Times*

The Perfect Wrong Note

Originally published in hardcover by Amadeus Press in 2003

Paperback edition published in 2006 by Amadeus Press
512 Newark Pompton Turnpike, Pompton Plains, New Jersey 07444

ISBN 1-57467-145-6

Printed in the United States of America

Illustrations by Angela Adams

The Un-Master Class® is a registered service mark (U.S. Patent and Trademark Office, Reg. No. 2,268,669).

Excerpts from *Lost in Translation*, copyright © 1989 by Eva Hoffman, used by permission of Dutton, a division of Penguin Putnum, Inc.

While every effort has been made to trace copyright holders and obtain permission, this has not been possible in all cases; any omissions brought to our attention will be remedied in future editions.

Library of Congress Cataloging-in-Publication Data

Westney, William.
  The perfect wrong note : learning to trust your musical self / William Westney.-- 1st original hardcover ed.
      p.   cm.
Includes bibliographical references (p.   ) and index.
ISBN 1-57467-083-2
1. Music--Performance. 2. Music--Instruction and study.
I. Title.

ML457.W47 2003
781.4--dc21

                                                    2003012792

A catalog record for this book is also available from the British Library.

www.amadeuspress.com

To the spirit of Eloise

Contents

Acknowledgments

Those I wish to thank:

for indispensable help with the manuscript: Danny Mar and Angela Adams for expert artwork and graphics, Marilyn Westfall, Mary Kogen, Seymour Fink, and Emilia Westney for feedback on the text, and especially editor Eve Goodman of Amadeus Press—skilled, patient, thorough, and always encouraging;

for helping me learn essential lessons along the way: Leopold Mittman, Donald Currier, Claude Frank, Paul Baumgartner, Eloise Ristad, and—most notably—all the students and workshop participants over the years who have entrusted me (and each other) with their thoughts and feelings, their efforts, and their honest responses;

for offering creative ideas and asking good, penetrating questions when I needed to hear them: associates Julia Scherer and Monica Hebert and family members Rich, Mary, Hazel, and Eve;

for significant professional assistance that helped make this book possible: The Paul Whitfield Horn Endowment of Texas Tech University, Anthony Tommasini, Kenneth Ketner, Seymour Fink;

for incalculable gifts: Ann and Dick Westney;

and finally—for unwavering support, treasured companionship, and belief in me throughout this project and all that has led up to it: Emilia, Ben, and Paul.

Preface

What could be sweeter than making music—trustingly, naturally, with confident ability, absorbed in each moment of pure expression? Humans are musical beings; to make music is our magical birthright and an important component of who we are and what brings us together.

What could be sadder than to forfeit that birthright? To love music and set out to make it one's own, only to be thwarted by fears, conflicts, tensions, and misconceptions? Ironically, this has been the experience of millions in industrialized societies, especially those who've had formal music lessons.

That loss shouldn't be happening, and that's why I've written this book. Music study can offer fulfillment for a lifetime. The pathway to success is simple; all we really need is an open mind, a realistic outlook, and some common sense.

Whether you are a student (of any instrument including the voice, at any developmental point from beginner to advanced), a teacher, a parent, a professional musician, or an ex- or would-be musician of any age, I invite you to join me in taking a clear-eyed look at the processes of music performance. Achievement in music depends on the philosophy we bring to it. A wrong note, for example, can indeed be "perfect"—beautifully constructive and useful—when we consider it thoughtfully. And doing so can lead to liberation and mastery.

With this possibility in mind, we will focus especially on how we approach practicing and performing, two activities that can be so worthwhile, fascinating, and pleasurable. Let's ask ourselves if our habitual ways are truly effective, encouraging, and worthy of the good intentions we bring to the pursuit of music.

Certain themes run through this book. We can reawaken our own vital instincts and trust them more. Free ourselves from thoughts that might hold us back. Act on our own perceptions, moment to moment. Believe in—and relish—our innate, proven ability to master complex new skills. Tap into our natural wisdom about the actual meaning of imperfections and mistakes—essential ingredients of solid learning.

As we consider lessons, let's have the courage to rethink their fundamental purposes, procedures, and the assumptions behind them. Admittedly, this isn't easy to do in a field that is so strongly based on traditions, and that prides itself (rightly) on keeping precious traditions alive. But I believe that some of our educational traditions have proven to be less than healthy to mind, body, and spirit, and have needlessly disheartened generations of music students. Instead of questioning the traditions themselves, though, many of those students simply ended up feeling that they'd failed, concluding ruefully that they were just not talented enough.

Some have nurtured their musical spirit by going in creative new directions, forgoing all rigorous or technical ambitions in favor of looser, less exacting styles of expression. But while any musical style can bring great artistic satisfaction, there is definitely a unique sense of personal fulfillment and achievement that can come from meeting—and succeeding at—the technical and artistic challenges of classical training. So it concerns me whenever I hear of someone giving up on such challenges for what seem to be the wrong reasons.

I begin the book by exploring the almost universal presence of a joyous and enthusiastic response to music in young children. Then I track what may happen to that musical vitality over time. Performance study and its traditions are examined, both in general terms and in detail. I take a look at breakthroughs—moments of discovery, transformations—and at how inspiring they can be, and I suggest ways in which they might be encouraged to happen more often. I delineate what's healthy in the music studio, in every sense, and include practical ways to avoid playing-related injury. Throughout the book there are references to the pull of ego and examples of how ego can disrupt our progress and distort our perceptions on many different levels. This ego-trap has a positive side, though; liberating ourselves from ego-centeredness through the study of music brings a rich philosophical and spiritual dimension to our learning, and this is the topic of the last chapter.

A special chapter (chapter 10) is devoted to the older recreational musician—anyone starting music or returning to it as an adult. Such a person often has enormous untapped potential but may also have some music-related issues from the past to deal with. I've spoken with hundreds of people in mid-to-late career, or newly retired, who are perfectly poised to blossom in the study of music. They have spare time, financial resources, curiosity, a hunger for personal artistic fulfillment, and a mature fascination with the transcendent powers of music. More importantly, having built careers and relationships, they have learned much over the years—in uniquely personal ways—about problem-solving, realism, risk-taking, and the zesty "Aha!" of insight and discovery. They've learned the difference between surface knowledge and deeper understanding. Yet even with all these advantages, many are reticent to take up music. They feel inadequate and leery; perhaps they lack confidence because of unsuccessful early lessons or performances. Many find that their thoughts about music making are in conflict; as one acquaintance put it, performing music has always been her "greatest desire and greatest fear." I hope this book will have a fresh, encouraging message for life-long learners, and that it will offer useful tips on how to develop a fruitful teacher-student relationship.

Ultimately, though, does it really matter whether we study music? Why make an issue of it? Simply put, music can help us feel joyful and complete. Humans in every culture cherish the musical impulse, love to share the musical experience, and sense its uncanny power to penetrate effortlessly to our very core and to unite us. Thanks to its abstract relationships, music provides flashes of insight that words can never translate. Thanks to the sensuous physicality of its rhythms, vibrations, colors, shapes, and harmonies, music invites us to respond body and soul to patterns greater than we are. Most importantly, the ever-changing stream of our emotional existence finds its perfect, truthful, and universal mirror in the flow of great music. This is why it's so fulfilling to "lose ourselves" in music.

Looking at it another way, rigorous music study is good for us. It offers bracing opportunities for growth. At the same time, it's a perfect form of working meditation—detailed, absorbing, intriguing, always different from one day to the next. To meet its demands requires a certain detachment, keen observation, and willingness to grasp information in often surprising ways. Sometimes it takes courage. Musical learning coordinates different parts of a person: body and mind, right and left brain, and expressive originality.

Since many spiritual traditions seek just such a synthesis of mind, body, and spirit, and just such a transcendence of the limitations of self, music practice can indeed be thought of as a spiritual practice of a certain kind. Interestingly, modern science is curious about the very same sorts of phenomena; integrated mind-body constructs of the human system are now coming to the forefront of cognitive research. So the processes of music making may have more to teach us collectively than we ever suspected, especially when those processes are working well.

The ideas I offer here have emerged over time, from various experiences I've had as a concert pianist, instrumental teacher, consultant, and workshop presenter in group settings throughout the United States and abroad. Along the way I had the good fortune to meet and work with author-presenter Eloise Ristad (1926–1985) during the last year of her life. The insights of this extraordinary person helped crystallize my thinking on several key points, and to point me in new directions. Lecture attendees and workshop participants have asked me repeatedly if a book is available that delves further into the approach I've presented to them, and into the breakthroughs that some have experienced. This book is my response to those requests.

Whenever possible I've illustrated the concepts with examples and references from outside the realm of music. We musicians have a tendency to become a bit isolated in our focus, and it's interesting to gauge the soundness of an idea by seeing how wide-ranging its applications are. My overall hope is to offer a down-to-earth approach that will be immediately useful and heartening to readers, as well as a vision of the healthy satisfaction through lifelong study that music can so naturally provide.

Dr. Benjamin Spock once reassured millions of new parents with the unforgettable opening words of his revolutionary book on child care: "TRUST YOURSELF: You know more than you think you do." That's exactly what I wish to convey about our musical adventures, wherever they may take us.

1 | *Music, Magic, and Childhood*

How did I end up becoming a professional pianist? By *not* starting my musical journey with piano lessons.

Instead I had the great good luck to be sent at the age of three to introductory music classes called Dalcroze Eurhythmics, named for the trailblazing Swiss educator Émile Jaques-Dalcroze (1865–1950). What Dalcroze understood—and demonstrated to be true for people of any age and at any music level from the most basic to the most sophisticated—was that musicality is essentially a whole-body experience.

These sessions didn't feel like instructional classes at all. Instead, they offered a lively, inviting world of colorful activity and humorous games; it just so happened that the games all had to do with music, and with integrated, specific responses to it. No practicing was required, no performing, no note-reading, no product of any sort—but there was deep, effortless learning.

Three-year-olds may not be the most orderly bunch, but they're loaded with energy, high spirits, and fun. They are excited by challenging games. They love activity, they express themselves vividly, they're endlessly curious, and they eagerly explore their physical surroundings. In a good Dalcroze class, all this natural vitality is skillfully channeled into musical understanding. Our favorite games focused on quick responses—physical and instantaneous—to changes in the music; these changes might consist of loud to soft, sudden accents, or abrupt shifts in melodic direction. To hear and respond in the same instant, without any preparatory signal, seems absurd, because at first it's almost impossible. Even at the age of three we sensed the silliness of such an attempt. The instructors liked to surprise us, to try to trick us, and we relished the humor of that. But kids are quite good at this game, thanks to their quick reaction time, and we prided ourselves on mastering the challenges, catching even subtle changes. Imagine the focused, attentive musical excitement, the joyous involvement, of a roomful of toddlers—giggling, their mischievous eyes shining.

Now picture a different scene, domestic and commonplace—not a music class at all. A three-year-old happens to be alone in a room. Music is playing on the stereo, and it's music with lots of rhythmic life and vigor to it. The child loves the music. How does she respond? (And I'm not thinking of a specially "talented" child, or future Juilliard virtuoso, just a typical three-year-old.)

From experience, we all know what's likely to happen: she will bounce and gyrate, embodying the pulsing energy of the music. And what if the next song on the album is a slow, melancholy one—will the toddler notice and respond somehow to the change? Yes, instead of bouncing she might croon and gesture dreamily along with the recording. To be

> *Toddlers and performing artists share this marvelous knack for open involvement.*

sure, the bouncing may be inexact, the crooning off-key, but what's wonderful is the unabashed openness and immediacy of that natural musical response evinced by so many children.

And if adults happen to witness the scene, without the child's being aware of it—what is their response? Blissful smiles all around. There is real purity and contagious joy in such un-self-conscious participation in music, and we adults sense it (and perhaps feel a bit of nostalgia). Once, of course, we were each that same bouncing toddler.

While you hold in your imagination these scenes of three-year-olds totally immersed in each musical moment, think about the opposite end of the spectrum—great, expressive musical artists. Picture a legendary performer you especially admire in a compelling moment of music making, doing what he or she does best at the violin or piano or on the opera stage. Again, there is total involvement, every fiber, sinew, and nerve-ending alert to the musical impulse, with none of the stiff reserve of so many students. I believe toddlers and performing artists share this marvelous knack for open engagement. In most three-year-olds, there is a rich wellspring of musicality just waiting to be tapped.

The effect of lessons

It's the students at later stages in life that I worry about. At times they seem to have lost that vital connection. The reason I count myself lucky not to have started my earliest music learning with piano lessons is that in those days lessons usually meant sitting still, facing front, not fidgeting, keeping my tiny fingers from making mistakes—and reading and counting at the same time! With so many tricky tasks to keep track of, chances are I would have simply been too preoccupied to enjoy the music with my whole being.

Far too often, though, a child who shows an affinity for music is shipped off right away (with the most optimistic of intentions) to instrumental lessons—in many cases piano lessons. There, the game often turns out to be radically different. Although the natural musical responses of the jumping toddler were visceral, spontaneous, and whole-body, now she must sit and think. She senses little connection between her own physical exuberance and the mathematical, symbolic abstractions on the page. The fingers—hard to control for young children—are as far away as they can be from the solar plexus, where music truly lives for the toddler (and anyone else, for that matter). Learning can be slow and frustrating, the student may become reluctant, and the distressing family battle about practicing often begins.

Now she is expected to show results every week. Her overloaded brain feels heavy because there seem to be so many ways to be wrong—wrong fingering, wrong note, wrong counting—that when things do go right she feels more relief than excitement. Soon, what began as an enjoyable musical exploration shifts entirely in its focus. Some traditional lessons imply an extramusical agenda to the student: discipline, self-control, meticulousness, persistence, and obedience. Interestingly, a cultural consensus seems to subscribe to this profile of music study, because many individuals, who know little about music themselves, have told me most emphatically and countless times over the years that what music lessons primarily teach is—discipline.

Of course self-discipline, persistence, and attentiveness do play a central role in mastering musical skills. We must be careful, though, not to think of music lessons in either-or terms. If we risk quashing musical vitality in the interest of discipline, we may certainly pay too high a price. Perhaps this isn't a real dichotomy; a person with vitality ends up doing *everything* better, more creatively—including systematic tasks like working out detailed fingerings. In any event, since I teach mostly college-age students, I see in those students the long-term results of their childhood experiences. In far too many cases, by the time the reliable prize-winner arrives in college, he has become so physically tense, expressively timid, and dependent on the teacher that he is at a developmental dead end, and his instrumental study must take a major detour before he can move forward. He may need to work with a teacher for a couple of years in ways that are much more like therapy than music study. But this "therapy" is a necessity if that person is to escape injury, rediscover his gusto, relax his body, and remember how to trust his own instincts and communicate the joy of musical response. Without that joyous connection to music, he will never be able to mature into an artist. In other words, he needs to get back in touch with his magical three-year-old self.

Toddlers, Martians, and Einstein

Magical is not too strong a word for a child's connection to music; there is extraordinary receptivity and lively creativity in young minds, and the results can be enchanting. Think of how small children often make up songs all day long, musicalizing their own experience and the world around them. (Maybe adults should try doing that too—very therapeutic!) Think of the surprisingly original, illogical, cute things they say, which the proud parents repeat—too often, no doubt—to their not-really-interested friends; it seems to me that the parents are genuinely inspired (and amused) by the startling viewpoints of children, so fresh and free. Everyone is delighted to be around such freedom of spirit, and in that sense a child's connection to music is magical.

Another trait of young children is the remarkably participatory nature of their mode of comprehension. I'm reminded of the term *grokking* (popular in the sixties), coined by science-fiction writer Robert Heinlein. In his novel *Stranger in a Strange Land*, Martians were all supposedly capable of "grokking," which denoted a fuller connection than "understanding" and was something for which a corresponding word in English didn't exist. The Martians apparently had something to teach humans in this regard:

> The Martians seem to know instinctively what we learned
> painfully from modern physics, that observer interacts
> with observed through the process of observation. "Grok"
> (literally "to drink") means to understand so thoroughly
> that the observer becomes part of the observed—to merge,
> blend, lose identity in group experience.[1]

This sounds to me like what three-year-olds do normally, especially in response to music.

Another attempt to describe in words that same mind-body openness can be found in a book by Bob Samples, *The Metaphoric*

Chapter 1

Mind. Samples makes a direct connection here to the creative genius of Albert Einstein, but he could just as easily be talking about artistry in general—certainly there is a musical element in the description.

> Children and infants seem deeply involved in the integra-
> tive mode nearly all the time. They do not restrict their
> sensory involvement to the aloof detachment that marks
> adultness—looking and poking. Instead they dive head-
> long into involvement. They immerse themselves in total
> sensory absorption of the issue. Touching, tasting, mim-
> icking, moving, dancing, and acting out the living and
> dying of whatever object, process, or condition they are
> confronted with is only natural. Sometimes their sensory
> involvement means a suppression of the major senses sim-
> ilar to meditative states. Meditative states in children are
> guised in the form of trance-inducing chants they often
> repeat over and over, and in the repeated body rhythms
> that seem to go on endlessly in the presence of exasperated
> adults. Daydreams are also a common form of child-
> meditation.
>
>   It is this unabashed acceptance—allowing all the iden-
> tifiable and some nonidentifiable senses freedom to be
> present—that led Einstein, as he explored the stratosphere
> of physical knowledge, to remark that most scientific
> advances involved a childlike joy. He and others said real
> discoveries were made because they reinstated ways of
> sensing that most had given up long ago.[2]

It is well known that Einstein believed that childlike intuition, free play, and body movement were integral to his creative thinking. Neurological researcher and educational specialist Dee Coulter of Naropa University (Boulder, Colorado) discusses Einstein's genius in her recorded lectures titled *The Inner-Dynamics of Creativity.*

20

According to Coulter, creativity has four components: Inner Gesture, Rigor, Incubation, and Composition. Of these four, the most crucial is the first stage, Inner Gesture—a natural ability for most small children, both musically and in other contexts. Inner Gesture is the "felt sense" of an idea, an empathic body connection to the shape and movement of that impulse. Later, the gesture may express itself as a verbal idea. Musical games like those of Dalcroze Eurhythmics evoke a core response that is very like what Coulter describes as Inner Gesture.

Einstein stayed wide open to such sensations, whereas the rest of us learn to ignore them in favor of logical reasoning much of the time. Einstein was asked what it felt like to get a great new idea in physics: did he know when one was coming? Certainly, he said, and the first sign was a muscular sensation throughout his body. Then came images, then some words to describe them, and finally the mathematical formulation would take shape. Looking at this creative sequence, says Coulter, we'd have to conclude that "the mind is located in the body."[3]

Einstein is by no means the only scientific innovator to say that physical involvement—and music—were crucial to the process of discovery. For his book *Inventors at Work*, Kenneth Brown interviewed prominent inventors about their creative methods. Stanford Ovshinsky, holder of more than one hundred patents in the semiconductor field, alludes to the need for "perfect pitch" and "physical intuition" in the process of assessing whether a new idea is worthy. Steve Wozniak, co-inventor with Steve Jobs of the Apple Computer, says, "Everything I ever read about an artist or a musician, the steps they went through, was equivalent to the mental steps I was going through. . . . Invention, like art, is kind of an idea that can't be seen, yet you have to express it some way. Back then, I knew I was like a musician or artist."[4]

Although we may not all be Einsteins, we do sometimes trust our bodies in quite a similar way. For example, we might say, looking back at a perplexing decision we had to make, "I considered all the alternatives and this one simply *felt right*." Or when we are struggling to understand a new concept, "I tried over and over to wrap my brain around it, but then it all just *fell into place*" (and we can feel that happening—somewhere deep in the body). If you imagine yourself saying such things, you will also notice the strong sense of certainty about them; we trust the felt sense profoundly, as well we should. We trust the mind-body when it works as a unit. The problem is, we just don't tend to honor it enough or integrate it enough into our logical processes of thought.

Musicality, creativity, and cognition

The richness of childhood perception has been explored by many writers and theorists, in styles ranging from the clinical to the poetic, passionate, and mystical. This rich perception can then lead to comprehensive awareness, integrated knowledge, and original-ity. Musical response typifies and develops childhood's powers of receptivity.

The energized, fluid creativity of play, for example, is a child-hood treasure that is often lost later. People happily forget them-selves when they are absorbed in play, and at the same time they are acutely alert. Johan Huizinga, pondering the basic nature of our species, suggested that besides *Homo sapiens* (the Knower) and pos-sibly *Homo faber* (the Maker), "There is a third function, however, applicable to both human and animal life, and just as important as reasoning and making—namely, playing. It seems to me that *Homo ludens*, Man the Player, deserves a place in our nomenclature."

Huizinga's description of play uses a luxuriantly musical vocabulary:

It may be that this aesthetic factor is identical with the impulse to create orderly form, which animates play in all its aspects. The words we use to denote the elements of

play belong for the most part to aesthetics, terms with
which we try to describe the effects of beauty: tension,
poise, balance, contrast, variation, solution, resolution,
etc. Play casts a spell over us; it is "enchanting," "captivat-
ing." It is invested with the noblest qualities we are capable of perceiving in things: rhythm and harmony.[5]

The distinctive intensity of childhood sights and sounds is
evoked by choreographer Agnes De Mille in her memoir, *Reprieve*.
The book recounts the massive stroke De Mille suffered in her sixties, and how its aftermath changed her awareness in unforeseen
ways. Part of this was a rediscovery of intuitive childhood knowing:

> All sounds, particularly voices, were higher when I was a
> child, and clearer. They came to the ear fresher, as though
> they'd never before been heard—the sound of someone
> hammering, the slamming of a screen door, steps on a
> wooden floor, wheels, a call. . . . On those occasions when,
> as a child, I was sick, I didn't have to do anything at all but
> lie and look and lie and listen, and to know in my being
> what was going on.[6]

The link she describes between the remarkably keen hearing
of children and a special kind of knowing "in [one's] being" under-
scores again the importance of auditory (musical) responses in the
early years. That remarkable auditory ability also shows itself in
the uncanny ease with which young children can pick up a foreign
language with native accent, idiom, and inflection. Philosopher
Susanne Langer sees aspects of higher thought in this discerning
receptivity to sound, this sensitivity to expressiveness, asserting
that young children (unlike adults) "read a vague sort of meaning
into pure visual and auditory forms." Langer believes this fertile
openness enhances intuition, since a child's mind "grasps analo-
gies that a riper experience would reject as absurd."[7]

Creativity theories of Arthur Koestler and others are based on this same idea—that the greatest gift is the ability to fuse together supposedly unrelated things, things that by rights ought to belong to separate spheres of thought or perception. This has also been described as the "harmony of ideas."[8] Koestler cites the famous ancient example of Archimedes, puzzling over how to calculate the volume of an irregular solid, in this case an ornate golden crown. This seemed impossible, beyond conventional mathematics. But one day, as Archimedes was easing his body into the bathwater, he noticed how the water rose an exact amount. This led to the then-startling notion of equal displacement of volume, by which solids of any shape could be measured precisely for volume, using the simplest of means.

I mention Archimedes not only as a good example of free-associating thought, but also because his insight came at a moment of physical participation, using the whole body. This is exactly how musical understanding works in young children too—through whole-body involvement. By using musical games to activate that natural mind-body connection, we encourage overall creativity in the young. And undoubtedly, if we were to continue to respond physically to music throughout life, we would have a wonderful way to preserve that type of creativity. Educator Edith Cobb calls this physicality the "plasticity of response" and considers it "the genius of childhood."[9] And speaking of genius, Albert Einstein's descriptions of his own processes are again relevant. His daring physical curiosity led him to wonder, much as a three-year-old might, "What would it be like if I could take a ride on a beam of light?"—not analyze it, but take a ride on it. This daydream led to his General Theory of Relativity.

If these depictions of childhood magic are correct, then what happens to the magic? Are all of us non-Einsteins doomed to lose it? An interesting view of this question comes from architect and visionary Buckminster Fuller, who was often called a genius but rejected that notion, claiming that neither he nor anyone he knew was a genius; it was simply a matter of some people being less "damaged" than others.[10]

What can damage us? Categorical notions of learning that discount the value of intuition. Any approach that denigrates bodily and nonverbal knowing. My own children spent a couple of years in a progressive, nontraditional elementary school, and even there the parents were told how important it was to encourage their children to categorize everything in their environment at every opportunity: "Which things are round?" "Which is the biggest?" Like all the other parents I thought this was excellent advice at the time, and dutifully encouraged my kids to categorize whenever possible. This exercise does have good teaching value, but it's unfortunate if in the zeal to categorize we trample on—or ignore—those surprising, illogical connections children tend to make. Therefore I think we may need to relax that mission a bit, and respect a child's intuitive, illogical, integrative thoughts at the same time that we teach the necessary, conventional categories.

Thousands of years ago, Lao Tzu had a definite opinion on the subject of categories and conventional thinking:

> Leave off fine learning! End the nuisance
> Of saying yes to this and perhaps to that,
> Distinctions with how little difference!
> Categorical this, categorical that,
> What slightest use are they!
> If one man leads, another must follow,
> How silly that is and how false![11]

Educational theorist Jean Piaget was hugely prominent in teachers' college coursework and shaped the outlook of several generations of schoolteachers in the mid-to-late twentieth century. Although Piaget did honor the importance of physical participation in the context of science experiments and the like, he basically considered abstract logic and formal reasoning to be the crowning glory of thought and the skills to which all education should aspire. There was little room in Piaget's hierarchy for nonlogical insights or artistic individuality. Modern theorists such as Howard Gardner have expanded the categories of learning in fertile new directions, especially Gardner's popular formulation of "multiple intelligences" which include the musical and the kinesthetic. But Piaget shaped many of us through our schoolteachers and continues to have an influence. From a pragmatic point of view, as well, intuitive insights are problematic because they can never be reliably measured or graded, while correct answers can be; thus schooling, by its very nature, may ignore intuition until it begins to wither away.

A precious resource

If in fact schooling has stifled someone's intuition, music can definitely have a restorative effect. Musical experiences—so accessible in childhood—are among the most integrative a person can have. It is quite striking how many musical terms appear in general descriptions of creativity: harmony, rhythm, shape, orchestrating the senses, dance, metaphor, abstract patterns, felt sense, and so on.

> *Musical experiences—*
> *so accessible in childhood—*
> *are among the most integrative*
> *a person can have.*

But the spark of musical spontaneity is delicate and easily extinguished. To snuff it out may be to diminish some other potentialities too, such as creative thinking or scientific innovation.

And finally, let's consider the link between childhood and adult musical performance. I believe that real artistry is based, in some fundamental way, on one's having preserved the three-year-old's relationship to music—losing oneself in it, becoming it, "grokking" it, sharing it. To be sure, there is always a risk of romanticizing this notion or making the equation too simplistic; a child's range of expression is nothing like an adult's, and an adult understands far better what the artistic conventions are and thus what sort of individual liberties he is taking.[12]

Nevertheless, a performer who responds with his entire self, not just his thinking mind, can create art of transcendent spirituality. Not only is the artist as open as a child is, but the constraints of individual ego and personality seem to dissolve in the act of performance. Putting personality aside opens the way for greater artistry. As mystical writer Krishnamurti put it, "Where there is total absence of yourself beauty is."[13] A sign of a great performance is that the audience begins to wonder whether it is the artist performing the piece or the piece performing the artist. Has the artist "mastered" the piece, or does it seem more like the artist is no longer a separate being, but is merging somehow with the music?

Adult music-making can closely resemble the blissful, trance-like, tactile absorption we once knew as toddlers. The easiest way for me to recall that state is to think of what it was like to play in a sandbox or at the beach, solemnly adding water and methodically making mud-pies, mesmerized by the feel of water, sand, and mud. No matter how old we get, there is something uniquely precious in that which we fabricate with our own hands. In the words of J. M. Thorburn, "All the genuine, deep delight of life is in showing people the mud-pies you have made; and life is at its best when we confidingly recommend our mud-pies to each other's sympathetic consideration."[14]

2 | *Vitality*

What becomes of the vitality that is so natural in childhood? This, of course, is the great question, and the answers to it can be poignant.

Sometimes musical vitality blossoms into vivid expressivity as a person grows up. Sometimes it is taken for granted, or its exuberance is dismissed as babyish. Sometimes it gradually withers away from neglect. Sometimes it is flattened by the insensitive remarks of a teacher, parent, or peer. In any event, vitality seems surprisingly perishable, despite its naturalness, and it requires nurturing in order to thrive.

Judgments and competition

I ponder the issue of vitality every time I find myself adjudicating local piano auditions; typically the students range in age from six or so up through high school. At the end of the day I look back and think, "Whose playing really reached me, made me feel something and respond?" And most of the time the answer is the six-year-olds. They have an innocent zest for playing itself, their sound is often strong and straightforward, they delight in what their bodies can do, and they are individualists. I remember one little guy who was so pumped about playing "Round the Wigwam"—his favorite piece—that he started whomping out those raucous open-fifth drumbeats in the left hand before he'd even finished sitting down on the bench. What eagerness! Clearly, he loved to play it, loved to share it and show off, and every molecule of him was part of that powerful musical energy and intent. His connection was honest and real; it radiated without self-consciousness. That's vitality.

By the time the teenagers arrive, however, things are quite different, and the difference is troubling. The various high-schoolers tend to sound uncannily alike. A fifteen-year-old girl starts to play *Für Elise:* her tone is thin and watery, her rhythm is limp, and while the localized gestures of her hands and wrists have clearly been schooled a certain way, the rest of her body seems rather slack and inert. Yes, there is careful shaping of phrases, consistent observation of the marked dynamics—all of which has the air of being carefully taught (to please the judge!)—but none of it seems to relate to her personally. The performance is wistful and apologetic, lacking conviction.

Of course, undeniable societal pressures and developmental issues can cause a fifteen-year-old to be more self-conscious than a six-year-old. All things considered, I'm sure it's a lot more fun to be six! Adolescents tend to be conformist, self-conscious about their bodies, and excruciatingly aware of public scrutiny (real or imagined). But the musical difference seems to go beyond that. If this shyness is only an adolescent phase, why doesn't the phase pass? I ask this because in many cases the musical plateau for life is reached during the teen years; this is when many people get stuck, stop improving, lose interest, and quit; and thus the book closes on their musical adventures.

When adolescents play without much conviction, they may be aware that despite years of lessons, their fundamental ability has not grown much recently. All they know for sure is that they've learned a new set of pieces each year. Even though the pieces now contain more overt technical demands, such as rapid scales and arpeggios, their playing may not have acquired new skills to meet these demands. When this is the case, they exude less sureness and enjoyment at the instrument than they used to, sensing (rightly) that the pieces are somewhat over their heads, and feeling a bit like impostors. One bright teenager told me that she had quit lessons because practicing had become so frustrating; not only was it repetitious, but it didn't seem to help all that much, especially when she compared it to the way her efforts reaped predictable rewards in school and other endeavors. I had to admit this seemed a perfectly sensible reason to stop.

So perhaps the fifteen-year-old who appears to have lost vitality is simply not terribly proud of her playing—she too may sense that something basic is lacking. Frequently, though, no one comments directly on what's lacking, since judges and teachers often make a point of being only kind and encouraging and are understandably careful not to offend other teachers. But in a strange way that reticence almost makes the situation worse, since she may end up thinking dejectedly, Well, that was obviously mediocre. If no one's saying anything, I guess that's all I'm capable of; I knew all along I wasn't very good at this!

Yet at the age of three she probably jumped, bounced, and made up songs with the best of them; and when piano lessons started she tackled her first pieces with spirit. But now she will likely quit music before long—and who can blame her?

On one occasion, I was asked to judge a group of eight fourteen-year-olds, all playing the same official contest piece. The piece's title was something like "South Sea Island," and it used rippling arpeggios and colorful pedaling to create sensuous sound-images of ocean waves and exotic aromas. The piece wasn't very difficult to play, and was clearly designed to give young players an exhilarating sense of how effectively the piano can be used to paint a lush aural picture. But it was hard for me to choose a winner, because to my dismay the contestants all played the piece almost identically: strict counting, mathematically consistent arpeggios, calculated and precise pedaling and dynamics—just the correctness a judge would supposedly want. But not one ocean wave did I hear or see, no sea breezes did I sense. I asked myself, Can it possibly be that out of a group of eight teenagers, not one has an active imagination? I knew that couldn't be so, but evidently their imaginations (quite lively at fourteen, no doubt) had no connection with playing the piano or music lessons. My worry, of course, is that by the time these kids get to college, very little in their approach to music will have changed. Many will still associate the piano so strongly with this repressed way of playing that to reprogram themselves becomes quite a difficult task.

Ironically, this squelching of the imagination was done for *my* sake, or for whoever happened to be the judge that day, even though robotic correctness is the last thing most judges want to see or hear. During the early years of study, correctness is often the focus, pleasing the judge is important, and in some cases little more is asked of the student. Sometimes signs of originality and spirit, such as experimentation and improvisation, are sternly suppressed by teachers, as countless adults have told me from their own frustrated memories. The theory seems to be that everyone ought to master the "basics" first; and later, the good stuff—personal connection to the notes, spontaneous feeling, imagination—can be added, like icing on a cake. (This is another commonly held notion that has been expounded to me repeatedly, even by people with no personal experience of music study.) But that's not a very good plan. When the day finally arrives that we've mastered enough basics, will the spark of vitality still be there?

Which skills?

Some years ago I attended an interdisciplinary conference called "The Biology of Music Making," which focused on the mind-body connection from different perspectives. During the presentations I became aware of a key semantic problem having to do with the slippery word *skill*. References to "musical skills" apparently had quite different meanings to different speakers, yet we acted as if there were no discrepancy, as if the term were consistent in meaning. No attempt was made to define the word or to find other words, and the confusion grew. Our understanding of what we mean by skill is important since it leads inevitably to a larger issue: what are we trying to accomplish in the study of music?

Some presenters at the conference were clearly referring to operational or what I would call outer skills—specific functional abilities such as intonation, finger dexterity, ear training, memorization, counting, and so on. In this context, the goal of music education is a general level of competence, acquisition of such skills as reading music, playing the right notes, carrying one's part in the choir, keeping time, following a conductor. The strategic question for educators, then, was how best to attain such competencies, which by and large can be readily evaluated.

Yet some presentations centered on another dimension entirely—integrative, intuitive connections to music, or "inner" skills. We heard case histories of musical improvisation used as a dramatically effective therapeutic technique for severe emotional disturbances. We heard inspiring heartfelt performances by untrained children from various cultures throughout the world. We learned about the fulfilling role of musical expression in the inner life of the dyslexic, the mentally challenged, and the child prodigy. The audience reaction gave clear testimony that these reports were thrilling and moving to everyone, and of great importance. Yet these transcendent, noncategorizable abilities are largely unrelated to schooling, or to the development of the usual testable, measurable skills of competence.

Inner and outer skills are not the same, nor does one automatically foster the other. The music education profession might do well to ponder this issue and to decide with more clarity what its goals are. High-school clarinetists march up and down the football field, for example, executing a complex routine with perfect regimented cadence. Their performance skills have been exhaustively drilled, yet they discover the next year in college music classes that other basics are undeveloped—they may have trouble singing on pitch, harmonizing, or even counting securely on their own. Inner skills, such as personal expressivity and creativity, are often dormant as well. Basically, these students have yet to connect with music.

One remedy would be to take a close look at the language used in judging student contests. I remember when I first started judging years ago, I was given a form to fill out for each student, with a grid that listed the basic elements: articulation, dynamics, pedaling, stylistic interpretation, rhythm, and even (occasionally) personal grooming. Not surprisingly, I would often hear performances seemingly tailored to that list: well-groomed, meticulous, dutiful, and—in my opinion—lifeless. I can see, however, the potential value of a checklist; it can help students to get specific feedback, and it can remind judges to be thorough. Yet according to the traditional checklist, even the most uninvolved player can easily score "Excellent" or "Superior" on most of the individual items. This is the problem with checklists and reductionist thinking. Nowhere on the grid could I find the juiciest, most indispensable traits, such as energy, individuality, communication, zest, imagination, sensitivity, healthy physical connection with the instrument, rhythmic vitality. These "inner skills" are essential for musicians at *any* stage, and they are well within the reach of even the elementary student.

Why not list them, or at least a few of them, on the judging form? Then we'd be framing clearly what's most valuable, for performance and for the students' own fulfillment. Students and teachers might then have a new focus, new goals, and a revamped idea of "what the judges want." For some teachers, of course, these priorities would not be new at all, and those teachers would undoubtedly be delighted to see them listed so prominently.

It might seem that the traditional criterion of "interpretation" would cover all those vital qualities, but in my view it doesn't quite suffice. Any judge can deem an interpretation to be stylistically correct or incorrect without commenting on whether there's actually any life in it. Similarly, the rhythm may be scored as correct but still lack that most enlivening musical quality of all: rhythmic *vitality*. How will classical music survive if it's not performed with immediacy and verve?

In the area of assessment, we should again avoid either-or thinking. A new checklist would still provide plenty of room for standard criteria such as pedaling, accuracy, and articulation. And I'm certainly not advocating lower standards of execution; no one likes to hear sloppy playing. But the organizers of music competitions—teachers, judges, and parents—have the power to set the tone of local events for everyone involved. The results could be refreshing.

Lessons and traditions

Like it or not, we live in a world of media images, and those images both reflect and create our cultural attitudes, at least to a degree. Thus I was disturbed to see a large billboard advertising a California sports-equipment store with the following images: in the foreground, the quintessence of cool—a boy crouching daringly on an air-borne skateboard with helmet, knee-guards, Day-Glo wristbands, all the gear needed for risky "extreme" sports; in the background, for contrast, epitomizing the uncool and boring: a bespectacled boy seated studiously at the piano. Ouch! According to this iconography, vitality and piano lessons are obviously worlds apart.

It certainly seems unfair. But doesn't it behoove us to pay attention and to ponder whether the picture might have a kernel of accuracy?

35

One cultural starting point for our investigation might be an adult social gathering, like a dinner party. I've found that if I happen to mention in the course of party conversation that I teach piano, the reactions around me are often fascinating. I'll see ironically amused or frankly pained expressions on some faces, and (perhaps after the second glass of wine) poignant individual stories may be unveiled. "Oh, I had lessons once,"

> "Oh, I had lessons once," someone will say, "but—"

someone will say, "but—" and the sentence might end in several ways: "I was never good enough," "I fell apart in the recital and never got over it," "It stopped being fun and I never touch the piano any more," "I quit and never should have, so I've told my kids I'm not going to let them quit." These are the frequently recurring themes, and the underlying sense of loss runs deep, despite the pose of amused detachment.

Leeriness of lessons shows up in our humor. Popular radio monologist Garrison Keillor spins a yarn of mid-America reminiscence in which he drives up the street where his childhood piano teacher once lived. The appreciative chuckles begin to build in the studio audience—they know quite well where this is going. Sure enough, he goes on to describe the feelings that set in as soon as he turns the corner onto that street: pounding heart and shallow, panicky breathing—guilt and fear. The audience guffaws heartily; everyone can relate.

Many times parents of musical toddlers have expressed to me their suspicion of lessons, often based on their own childhood experiences. They cherish the freedom with which their child sings himself to sleep and beats out rhythms on every saucepan—but, they ask, will lessons take the joy out of all that and make him musically bored and self-conscious? This is a poignant, perceptive question indeed.

In heartbreaking fashion, an anonymous writer has chronicled the loss of artistic vitality through lessons. This memoir was published not in a music journal but in a grass-roots literary magazine. The magazine regularly prints readers' contributions on an announced topic, and in this case the general topic was prisons. As a music teacher I was stunned by the entry:

Prisons

Drawing, writing, and dancing were once a part of me.
I felt no fear when I picked up a crayon. I didn't retreat
when music asked me to dance.

Then I found myself in dance classes, art classes, violin
lessons. Soon there were expectations to fulfill; the effort
became joyless. My mind might trick me into revealing I
wasn't smart enough. My body could trap me into betraying
that I was not a dancer, not a musician, not an artist—that
I was nothing. My drawings, poems, the pull of my bow
across the violin strings, all seemed inadequate. The violin
was a special instrument of torture, not self-expression.

It was time to retreat. I refused battles I was not sure of
winning. My drawings became mechanical; in the modern
dance and ballet classes I imitated the movements without
being in my body. I tried only when I knew I could do
something well, and went through the motions in everything else. No one saw what I was doing, including me.
Around the best part of myself I constructed bars so
strong I still can't break free.

What this prison needs is a riot—a knife held to the
throat of the jailer that is me.[1]

A grim account, sobering to any teacher in the arts (even though the writer doesn't seem to be blaming any teacher for the retreat). Could we possibly be having that effect on someone, and not be aware of it? From what people tell me, the answer is definitely yes, even when teachers have been pleasant and encouraging.

As classical musicians, we do tend to conserve traditions, hence the fitting name for our professional schools, "conservatories." We have the privilege of passing on a core of knowledge from person to person across the generations, knowledge that can't be found in any book or recording. We consider this our sacred mission, to be stewards of that precious tradition. During my college years, I was awed and excited to learn that my teacher (Mittman) had studied in Warsaw with Aleksander Michalowski, who in turn had been a student of Karol Mikuli, who studied with—Chopin! The art and craft were coming straight to me through that pipeline of apprenticeship, with only three human beings between me and Chopin.

But as in families, not everything that gets passed down is good, and it may not be wise to swallow tradition whole. As we shall see in the next chapter, traditional notions about practicing have—all by themselves—discouraged many students over the years, even when teachers have been quite supportive. When it comes to advanced teaching, though, one clearly unhelpful convention is that of the imperious, omniscient, temperamental maestro driving his students mercilessly, ridiculing their paltry efforts, and flinging the score against the wall in disgust, all out of devotion to high art. This stereotype may have become a Hollywood cliché, but it still contains a dose of truth.

In her 1880 memoir, *Music-Study in Germany*, the young American Amy Fay compiled her delightfully frank letters to the folks back home. In them, she recounted vividly her own experiences studying piano with Franz Liszt and other European luminaries of the nineteenth century. Here she describes the tempestuous first master-lesson she had with Karl Taussig, the revered Berlin pianist-pedagogue:

> He was as amiable to me as he ever can be to anybody, but
> he is the most trying and exasperating master you can

possibly imagine. It is his principle to rough you and snub
you as much as he can, even when there is no occasion for
it, and you can think yourself fortunate if he does not hold
you up to the ridicule of the whole class. You can imagine
what an ordeal my first lesson was to me. I brought him a
long and difficult Scherzo, by Chopin, that I had practiced
carefully for a month, and knew well. Fancy how easy it
was for me to play, when he stood over me and kept calling
out all through it in German, "Terrible! Shocking!
Dreadful! O Gott! O Gott!" I was really playing it well, too,
and I kept on in spite of him, but my nerves were all rasped
and excited to the highest point, and when I got through
and he gave me my music, and said "Not at all bad" (very
complimentary for him), I rushed out of the room and
burst out crying. He followed me immediately, and coolly
said, "What are you crying for, child? Your playing was not
at all bad." I told him that it was "impossible for me to help
it when he talked in such a way," but he did not seem to be
aware that he had said anything.[2]

That sort of patronizing obliviousness on the part of famous
teachers is still known to exist today, albeit in rather modified form.
But even when it is subtle, disrespectful treatment can easily cause
students to lose heart and (as a natural consequence) lose vitality.

Interestingly, Fay has quite a different impression of Franz
Liszt himself, whom she found to be an artist and human being of
surpassing greatness:

Nothing could exceed Liszt's amiability, or the trouble he
gave himself, and instead of frightening me, he inspired
me. Never was there such a delightful teacher! and he is
the first sympathetic one I've had. You feel so *free* with
him, and he develops the very spirit of music in you. He

> doesn't keep nagging at you all the time, but he leaves you your own conception. Now and then he will make a criticism, or play a passage, and with a few words give you enough to think of all the rest of your life. There is a delicate *point* to everything he says, as subtle as he is himself.[3]

Nurturing and humane, Liszt was clearly an exceptional teacher for his time.

Later pedagogues voiced more "modern" ideas about teaching, but hints of a fundamentally condescending attitude could still be found. An interesting figure in this regard is Tobias Matthay, a revered piano teacher in England during the early part of the twentieth century, considered an oracle of sorts by his devoted disciples. Matthay's innovative methods combined technique, musicality, and natural physical functioning into a successful package, and the trademark of his approach was a notable warmth of tone and phrasing.

Matthay's theoretical books on piano teaching are stimulating, opinionated, and also—in my view—somewhat self-contradictory. His viewpoints often seem impressively far ahead of their time; for example, he claimed in his book *Musical Interpretation* (1913) that "accurately speaking, we cannot 'teach' anyone anything—in the sense of our being able *directly to lodge* any knowledge of ours in another mind."[4] This presages the thought of psychologist Carl Rogers, who wrote nearly fifty years later, "Anything that can be taught to another is relatively inconsequential, and does not influence behavior significantly."[5]

In entertainingly graphic terms, Matthay expressed how futile lessons can be when a student remains passive, like "a laboratory funnel with its mouth widely gaping, ready to receive any chemicals (pleasant or otherwise) which the operating chemist may see fit to pour in." The student should be encouraged to think independently; otherwise, at the instrument he becomes "an automatic strumming machine." Teaching that tells the student exactly what to do and how to do it is not teaching at all, says Matthay, but "cramming," and of this he most strongly disapproves. But just a few pages later he advises:

> Instead of acting as a bad orchestral conductor, you must act like a good conductor at rehearsal, you must explain to your pupil the most intimate details of structure and feeling, so that he may be musically able to see and feel rightly and therefore play rightly.

Matthay continues:

> The difference between a good and bad orchestral conductor depends on the same laws: the bad conductor treats his men like machines . . . whereas the really great conductor tries to make his men into intelligent artists . . . tries to make them see the music.[6]

Thus while Matthay criticizes teachers who cram or force-feed information, he still seems to believe that students know very little, couldn't possibly have their own valid artistic impulses, and need to be made into something by the godlike teacher. This contradiction lives on (subtly) in certain teachers who advocate "independent thinking" leading to student "discovery," but always with the unspoken assumption that what the student discovers will be a pre-ordained, teacher-approved truth.

As a society, we're quite accustomed to the top-down hierarchy of traditional lessons—"teacher knows best"—even though this model can be less than satisfactory. Renowned violin pedagogue Dorothy DeLay, whose successful nontraditional and nurturing psychological approach helped attract the greatest talents in the world to her studio, describes her own early discouragement as a student:

I used to have teachers who tried to teach me by example,
and what they would do is say, "No, no, do it like this"; and
I would think, Well that is different from what I am doing,
but I can think of a hundred ways it is different. I wonder
which one they are talking about. I would try something
and the teacher would say, "No, no, do it like *this*," so I
would try it again, change it, do something else, and that
wouldn't be what was wanted either, and I would go home
very upset. I never could figure out which aspect of what
they had done was what they meant. It was the most frustrating experience I have ever had.[7]

An incident from my own experience mirrors DeLay's
account. I was studying in Europe and brought the meditative
slow movement of a Beethoven sonata to a lesson with my very
traditional and esteemed maestro. He seemed especially energized and zealous that day, and eagerly set out to mold my rendition of the sparsely
written first measure to
the highest artistic
purity. So he had me play
the same simple phrase

> *I felt my self-confidence oozing away—
> if this was such a breakthrough,
> why wasn't that obvious to me?*

over and over, suggesting minuscule adjustments in the shaping,
pacing, and tone quality of it, conducting me, singing along,
never quite satisfied, until at repetition forty-seven he burst out
in wild shouts of joy and exultation that I had finally *gotten* it!
The heavens had opened—except that I had no idea what made
that repetition different from all the others. All I knew was that
he loved it, because (presumably) that's just how he would play
it himself. Sitting there baffled, I felt my self-confidence oozing
away: if this was such a breakthrough, why wasn't that obvious
to me? Wasn't I gifted enough to sense genuine artistry in a

phrase? And what exactly had been so wrong with my first forty-six attempts?

Such experiences, if we survive them psychologically, can become a great inspiration to find new paradigms of teaching.

Much music teaching seems more concerned with controlling the student than with encouraging the student's own impulses. Constant controlling dampens vitality. Among the most influential music educators of the twentieth century was Shinichi Suzuki, founder of the innovative and internationally popular Suzuki Method. Primarily for string instruments, it is a total-immersion, "mother-tongue" approach that makes significant use of repetition and rote absorption. This in itself is highly effective, largely because it wisely allows young beginners to watch, listen, and imitate without always worrying about abstractions like note-reading and mathematical counting. Learning under the Suzuki Method also resembles the learning of spoken languages, with an immediacy reminiscent of Dalcroze Eurhythmics. A considerable amount of playing is done in groups, and Suzuki classes perform most impressively (for the proud parents) in a very short time.

Howard Gardner, the respected educational theorist, admires Japanese culture for its caring commitment to the young and to the arts; Japan is a society in which "tremendous attention is paid to the development of musical skill." He considers the teaching solidly successful—"Suzuki students travel amazingly far on the basis of shrewd teaching"—but immediately goes on to say that Mr. Suzuki himself thought of the training mostly as "character and discipline" rather than solely music. Gardner concludes, "Perhaps not surprisingly, most of his students cease playing at or before adolescence."[8]

This doesn't seem quite right—a method with a high percentage of skilled dropouts, yet it is deemed a success? How far did the students really "travel"? Perhaps they trained outer skills at the expense of the abiding inner ones. Teachers who have taken on former Suzuki students have told me that in some cases, especially if the student had stayed too long in the method, further progress becomes difficult. The students are used to passive absorption from mother, teacher, and the group, and they are used to easy public approbation. They are often unable to identify or solve an individual inner problem, or they lack the patience to grapple with a difficulty. Also, they have always played music exactly like the rest of their group, so the idea of a personal, spontaneous interpretation is alien and risky to them. In fact, advanced Suzuki classes sometimes listen over and over to a single professional recording of a work and are taught to mimic that rendition in every nuance.

Yet, ironically, spontaneous self-expression is the essence of Western music, and it also happens to be something which young children are already very good at by nature.

The good news is that so many kids really love to go to their Suzuki lessons. The (required) collaboration with one parent, the cheerful group socializing, the security and familiarity of the musical repetitions, all contribute to their enjoyment. And Suzuki performances by the very young can indeed be impressive in their accuracy, ensemble, and group charm. But sometimes the look in the young performers' faces is eerily blank and uninvolved, even while the group rides the crest of a well-rehearsed "expressive" crescendo.

Because most music lessons consist of an encounter between just two people, interpersonal psychology is bound to play a major role. A central reason the relationships between individual teachers and students can become skewed, off-balance, and teacher-dominated, is that the music studio is often the setting for a classic example of co-dependence: a lack of boundaries and of healthy psychological

And when we give up the futile notion that we are supposed to be always in control, and embrace instead the ever-changing nature of reality, we feel liberated. Musical performance can be tricky. Will our inconsistent attempts discourage us, or will the ups and downs end up yielding a fuller understanding? If we play a passage perfectly today, we may stumble tomorrow—this is quite normal, since in the arena

> *The good practicer tastes the vitality of adventure and the dramatic rewards of risk-taking.*

of performance nothing is permanent. But the reasons for the stumble can be figured out if we stay curious and don't take it personally. In most cases the stumble is a sign that some detail of the music, although learned to a degree, just needs to be integrated more fully.

Ultimately, by *giving up* the ego-driven illusion of control we actually *gain* a deeper, more serene sort of control, because more thorough learning will take place. This is the central insight about fruitful practicing, paradoxical as it may seem at first. Whether we clutch at control or release it willingly has a direct effect on our happiness and vitality—and this principle has implications well beyond the realm of music.

According to Buddhist teachings, impermanence itself can be a source of joy. As author Steve Hagen explains it, "Everything we look at, including ourselves and every aspect of our lives, is nothing but change. Vitality consists of this very birth and death. This impermanence, this constant arising and fading away, are the very things that make our lives vibrant, wonderful, and alive."[11]

3 | *Juicy Mistakes*

I've alluded many times to the traditional concept of practicing and lessons, so I should clarify what I mean by that characterization. The traditional view has evolved since the nineteenth century and encompasses a range of assumptions about how to reach musical goals and how to teach. I am most concerned, though, with the management of mistakes, or perhaps I should say those unexpected events we usually *label* as "mistakes."

As a reference for this aspect of traditionalism I've used *The Pianist's Problems* by William Newman, but many other sources say virtually the same thing. While you read these statements, ask yourself whether they seem correct to you:

- The mind-body system is like a computer, retaining with exactitude all the information it receives.
- Therefore, if we want accurate results, we must feed the system only accurate raw data.
- Even casual mistakes become learned permanently.
- Mistakes should be prevented, since they will eventually mess up everything.
- Mistakes can be prevented by hesitating, slowing down generally, playing with extra care.
- Mistakes are generally a sign of shoddy, inattentive practicing.

These words do contain a lot of truth, but they can mislead us too. That's what makes this analysis so tricky. Many of us have subscribed to the traditional approach and considered ourselves in agreement with its logic, only to discover later through direct experience that the traditional approach doesn't always work and may in fact create problems. This can be quite confusing and can cause us to blame ourselves needlessly. More clarity, then, is called for, and I hope to be able to provide a bit of that in the course of this chapter.

Newman's viewpoint is quite typical. He disparages what he calls the "mistake habit" and describes the "viciousness" of a natural system that automatically makes every wrong note into a new program, a permanent memory tape that will come back to haunt us. "Mistakes become learned and stick just as correct procedures do." As a corrective, he recommends a policy of "hesitate rather than err," claiming that "you can catch yourself before you make the mistake, just as you would if you found yourself about to walk off a cliff or run down a pedestrian." Forbidding images such as these contribute to an atmosphere of guilt right from the start, the implication that any musical mistake you make is your own fault, a disaster you should never have allowed to happen.

Interestingly, though, Newman casually pinpoints a central weakness of his own argument when he concedes that "anticipating the mistake in advance can be very difficult."[1] Yes indeed! Perhaps a mistake that's become a bad habit, something one has often done before, *can* be anticipated in the mind, but anticipating an honest, pure mistake is not only difficult, it's clearly impossible. And to hesitate in situation after situation is to set up an ongoing inner conflict. One feels "My body wants to do things but I mustn't let it," and this creates tension and impedes the flow of energy. Putting it simply, it's not much fun to hesitate and be careful all the time—and frankly it's hard to believe that hesitation could possibly be an effective pathway to virtuosity or freedom.

But let's put all that aside for the moment. Let's proceed in our imaginations to what happens next: at a lesson, after a week of practice in the mistake-free traditional mode.

The scenario: I'm a high school student who's been assigned three new pages of a Mozart sonata for my lesson next Tuesday. I've heard the elegant sonata before and am eager to get my hands on it. "Bring in the first three pages next week," says Madame X, my illustrious teacher. For the first couple of days I enjoy exploring, taking the music apart, trying to figure out the new material and get the feel of it.

But then next Tuesday begins to loom. What if I'm not ready on time? What if it's not perfect? It'll look like I haven't practiced enough, and what would Madame think of me then? I'd hate to let her down. She's always saying, "Remember the most important principles: always play musically, and be sure everything is 100 percent accurate *from the very beginning!*"—and I've *got* to have those three pages done. So I make myself find some way of getting through all of it even though in a sense I'm still sight-reading, and it's taking all my fiercest concentration to manage the new fingerings, dynamics, and rhythms all at the same time and try to be "expressive" as well! (But if I neglect any of the expressive markings, I know Madame is likely to pounce and call it to my attention with "Have you forgotten what *crescendo* means?") All I know to do is to keep repeating the piece over and over with care, in hopes that gradually my playing will become more confident. I focus some on the "hard parts," playing them slowly and meticulously, even working on each hand separately, but the results are less than inspiring. Well, at least I've carried out my assignment, dutiful student that I am. But I'm beginning to wonder whether I still like the piece, or if I'll ever be able to play it.

Off I go to Tuesday's lesson. Madame settles herself in her chair and opens her beloved volume of Mozart so she can follow my rendition measure by measure. I nervously clear my throat and proceed to labor through the three pages the best I can, thinking and concentrating as hard as I know how. Mustn't sully the sublime legacy of Mozart! The trouble is, after only one week every bar is somewhat shaky, hesitant, and unmusical, but it's as close to perfect as I seem to be able to make it. My clenched shoulders, wrists, and jaw bespeak the intensity of my concentration. I remember to observe all the interpretive markings. But I stumble badly in several places, much to my shame, frustration, and chagrin. I'm not used to hearing mistakes in practice, and I'm mortified to hear them now. "It went much better at home," I mumble quite truthfully, hating the apologetic helplessness of those words. But since there isn't a comfortable, enjoyable, or satisfying measure for me anywhere in the piece yet, all I have to cling to is the fact that I at least *tried* to do it all.

And what can Madame possibly say? Clearly I haven't yet given her much to work with; my rhythm is unsteady, my physical movements are self-conscious, my tone is colorless, I'm exuding general insecurity and not much musical personality. Madame sighs (am I wasting her time after all?), smiles thinly, but seems vaguely displeased and bored, and of course I'm somewhat embarrassed too (maybe I have no business being here, pretending I have real talent!).

Hoping to spur me on, she gives me her best critique, describes—or perhaps illustrates—majestic musical results that can be attained: how much more beautiful and singing the melody could be, how accurate and fleet the technique should be, how my body should flow, what dramatic contrasts one can achieve. She sends me home with unconvincing words about how I just needed to "work harder for next time" but had nonetheless made a "good start."

But have I made a good start? What exactly *have* I learned this week?

I learned to fear some great music that I really wanted to play. I learned to feel bad about my shaky and sluggish abilities, my slow progress. Deep down, I am beginning to feel inept and unmusical. I learned that my fingers could betray me, at just the worst moment. And I learned to blame myself for all of it. (Probably in years to come I'll say "Oh, I was lucky to get into the studio of a very fine teacher with European training, she played beautifully, had a lot to offer—but I just didn't have enough talent.") All the negativity I've learned will stick with me and be hard to overcome later, because that's how impressionable and programmable the mind-body system is.

Whew! Sounds pretty grim. In fact, though, weekly lessons often do far more harm than good, even when the teacher is absolutely well-meaning. Sometimes the very fact that there is a weekly lesson can be counterproductive. Why should it be assumed that the student's efforts will be ready for aesthetic critique after only seven days? Why

> *Weekly lessons often do more harm than good.*

should accuracy and control be expected right at the start, rather than at the end of the process? Many students, including me, have noticed that whenever the teacher went out of town for three weeks we made more progress than usual. Our learning process could unfold naturally over the three weeks, without the disruption of those premature attempts to perform every week.

Luckily, I received clues along the way that other philosophies were possible and could work better. The first clue came early; I was about seven years old when I got my first inkling that "mistakes" weren't always as negative as they seemed. It happened like this:

At the piano lesson I was playing a melodious little piece (simplified Chopin, as I remember) that I liked and had learned quite easily. I was enjoying showing it off for my teacher—Mr. Kleiman—with lots of expression. Suddenly I hit an obvious clinker in my right hand. It sounded stupid, and it made me feel stupid. That wrong note had never happened before. Embarrassed and annoyed, I started to play the phrase over again immediately so that I could really "fix" that note, erase the mistake. After all, I was my teacher's prize pupil, and I had a reputation to uphold!

To my surprise, Mr. Kleiman cut me off and said, "Hey, don't fix it; if you're going to make a mistake, why not make a nice, big, fat *juicy* one?"

Hmmm—say what? This caught me off guard and sounded ridiculous, but somehow it felt like great advice, even though I was too young to comprehend much about it. I sensed that he was telling me the right thing. And I'd certainly never heard a teacher say anything like that before. (It's always memorable when teachers do something unexpected.)

It worked too. As soon as he said it, I laughed. My shoulders relaxed. His words gave me permission to keep my energy flowing, to play with honesty. He was obviously asking me to experience that particular mistake fully, without scorning it (if the mistake was "juicy," how could it be bad?). If he hadn't interrupted me and had allowed me to make the impatient correction, I would have felt like a different person altogether—tense, disappointed with myself, grasping at control, desperate for approval.

> If the mistake was "juicy," how could it be bad?

By contrast, his advice (although it contradicted what most piano-pedagogy books say) told me "You're OK, you don't have to prove yourself to me—but what's that fascinating piece of evidence *out there?* What would happen if you didn't reject it, but embraced it instead?" When I tried the passage a few more times with this new attitude, my muscles, nerves, and mind didn't recoil or disrupt the natural sorting-out process, and somehow my note-problem solved itself very quickly. Undoubtedly there was a logical, legitimate reason why I had missed the note in the first place. My body figured it out in its own straightforward way, and the learning was secure and permanent. This differs sharply from the more typical "good-student" response: feeling shame, and then manipulating the note to be right, using subtle tension and willpower—just to make sure we look good to someone else.

words of Shakespeare (*Hamlet*), "There is nothing good or bad, but thinking makes it so." Let's explore two basic categories of mistakes as I've labeled them: honest and careless.

Honest mistakes

Rarely, if ever, are honest mistakes mentioned in pedagogical books—it's as if they didn't exist in the music studio. Yet the golden pathway to learning, not just in music but in anything in life, is through one's own, individual, honest mistakes. We all learn uniquely, so there is a unique pattern to the mistakes that each of us needs to make. These mistakes form the quickest way, the healthiest way, to learning that is authentic and solid. Best of all, the process of working through honest mistakes has vital, positive energy because it grows out of an attitude of healthy self-acceptance. Why waste energy feeling guilty for no good reason?

Before delving further, let's consider the word *mistake*. It may not be the ideal word, but it's hard to think of a substitute that's any better, so I continue to use it. Words, though, can be deceptive because of the perpetual problem that (as the famous saying has it) "the map is not the territory." Words are not the same as experience, and words often reduce experience simplistically, or interpret experience with a clumsy hand.

Mistake tends to imply something regrettable, something that shouldn't have happened. But if you meant to play an F and your finger struck a G instead, was that a mistake? You could just as easily call it something else: an unanticipated outcome or a surprising piece of new evidence or an intriguing event. All we know for sure is that at the moment you struck the G, you meant to do one thing and something different happened.

How can you tell if the mistake was an honest or a careless one? If you weren't paying attention at the time, and you didn't take the mistake seriously and deal with it immediately, it was careless, a mistake that will cause you trouble later on, just as we've always been told. But if you *were* paying attention and the mistake happened anyway, it's probably honest. Honest mistakes aren't caused by inattention; they're simply what happens when the body is allowed to express itself without restriction. If you take time immediately to process that mistake (which we will examine in the next chapter), your learning will be pure and lasting.

Each honest mistake wants to be allowed to process itself into correctness. It's frustrating not to do so. Oftentimes music teachers, in a sincere attempt to loosen up a tense or timid student, will cry out, "Just play any notes! Don't worry if you make mistakes!" But this doesn't tend to work well, because it is genuinely distressing for the student. How can it be freeing to play a lot of ugly wrong notes, if you just let them stand and don't let them convert themselves into rightness? After all, it *does* matter which notes we eventually play.

Among the most efficient uses of practice time is to produce as many honest mistakes as possible—intentionally. This gives us lots of excellent data. The method of producing them is simple: focus your intention, relax, execute the chosen segment with gusto, and pay close attention to the result. Repeat as needed. Don't take any of it personally. Trust the process and don't try to control it. Enjoy all the sensations.

Honest mistakes are not only natural, they are immensely useful. Truthful and pure, full of specific information, they show us with immediate, elegant clarity where we are right now and what we need to do next. This is why a particular wrong note can indeed be thought of as perfect. Honest mistakes save a lot of time. As I will illustrate, they often have a sophisticated knack for revealing the underlying, specific reason for a particular glitch—a reason the conscious mind may not have considered. Honest mistakes demonstrate that the body is smart in a different way from the intentional mind. Sometimes we have to experience fully what's wrong in order to

Honest mistakes give texture to the act of learning.

understand and integrate what's right, and honest mistakes are the only way to do that. They give texture to the act of learning.

The honest-mistake approach isn't so easy to accept for most adults, or for older children; we're driven too much by our emotional need to control events and avoid embarrassment. But luckily we can all share the same source of inspiration, one that's always available to us: we can think back to how we learned things at the very beginning, at the age of one or two. During those eventful early years we were expert practitioners—ardent devotees—of the honest mistake; therefore, no approach could be more natural to us.

Observing my own children as toddlers, I was in awe of the adventurousness and efficiency of their learning. At the same time, I began to better understand the flaw in traditional music pedagogy. Like all kids, mine made every gross "mistake" imaginable—falling down clumsily, crashing into tables, bringing the spoon to their noses, garbling their words. But their attitude was admirable indeed: focused, persistent, enthusiastic, and undeterred. They never felt a shred of guilt or self-consciousness when they missed the mark; instead they were innocently surprised, bemused, and endlessly fascinated by the results of their attempts. (Luckily for them, they had never read stern dictates by the likes of Mr. Gieseking.) Like any parent, I was all smiles and encouragement—"Ha ha! You broke the floor!"—not that they seemed to need much encouragement. Neither did they need any instruction; that was obvious.

Did they then program themselves into a lifelong tendency to crash into furniture and drop their food on the floor, having "permitted" so many mistakes to get programmed in? Clearly not. Every mistake was completely and efficiently processed ("So *that's* what it feels like to mash oatmeal into your nose!"), and a few weeks later I would be amazed at how much they had mastered, and how elegantly. The process may appear messy, depending on your point of view, but one thing is clear: *their honest mistakes left absolutely no residue.* And they couldn't have had all those breakthroughs without them.

Chapter 3

Careless mistakes

In my view, the identifying trait of the careless mistake is inattentiveness, both in how the mistake is made and in how we respond to it. Of course, there can be many causes for such inattentiveness. But if our initial intention in playing something is generalized and ill-focused ("Well, I'll just play through this new piece a few times and hope for the best"), followed by a generalized assessment of results ("That wasn't too bad, for something I just started two weeks ago"), we really have laid the groundwork for a future mess. Because of our casual intentions, we won't even notice some of the mistakes that happen. Others will just lie there, unprocessed, yielding no information at all. Having not been given a chance to correct themselves, they will indeed become unfortunate habits later on.

The careless mistake is one that gets rationalized, explained away. It's awfully tempting to explain away inadvertent mishaps in the practice room, but explaining events away is in itself a form of mental carelessness. Newman warns us not to casually "chalk up" mistakes to "human error," and I agree with him totally. This is a habit everyone should break. Here are a few examples of the rationalizing thoughts we're all so good at:

- That never happened before; I just wasn't concentrating.
- Well, nobody's perfect; even Babe Ruth struck out a lot.
- I got distracted.
- Sounds pretty good on the whole.
- I know this perfectly well—I don't know why I got so nervous!

Notice how narcissistic these thoughts are; they are all about me and how I want to look good and justify myself, while ignoring the useful, objective evidence at hand. Yet many books on practicing, including those that propound the integrated functioning of body and mind, actually encourage us to be mentally careless in this way and to explain away our wrong notes. These texts often place an exaggerated reliance on one holistic principle as the answer to everything. That wrong note wouldn't have happened, they might say, if you had only *heard* the note better in your imagination before playing it, or visualized it more exactly, or sensed the impulse more in your solar plexus, or connected to your inner sense of rhythm. So again the underlying message is: start feeling guilty, because it's all your fault!

Mistakes as teachers

Fortunately, babies and toddlers aren't the only ones who are in touch with the importance of realistic, juicy mistakes. In many areas of endeavor, we seem to share a common-sense understanding that risk-taking is absolutely essential for success. For example:

- Ice skating—if you want to master a double axel, be willing to fall on the ice a lot.
- Succeeding in business—be willing to fail a few times.
- Speaking a foreign language—plunge right in and say it the best you can; if you don't speak up because you might be wrong, you'll never learn.
- Mastery of cooking—make a few "creative" stews you'll have to feed to the dog.
- Learning to drive a stick-shift car—lurch forward, stall out, make a public spectacle of yourself (the instructor's frantic exhortations to "let out the clutch and give it some gas" mean nothing to you in your moment of panic). In a few days you'll be shifting smoothly like a pro.
- Riding a two-wheeler bicycle—first you decide that you're tired of being the only kid on the block who can't ride a

two-wheeler, so you open yourself to risk, thinking, "I don't care what happens, if I embarrass myself or skin my knee, I'm going to try it!" Someone runs alongside, holding the seat, and you find your balance, going faster and faster. This is fun! Now you quickly turn the wheel— and crash to the ground.

There's a sophisticated relationship between rate of speed and the ability to control a turn, and the body understands it beautifully as soon as the "mistake" is made. In fact, there's no other way to teach or learn this relationship—no lecture or explanation could ever come close. Everyone knows how this process works from experience; we don't even question it. Of course, even when it comes to bicycle riding we have personal choices: if we have an unusually high need to be in control we could just leave the training wheels on permanently and *never* figure it out.

And there are plenty of music students who have never removed the metaphoric training wheels from their performing. But in music, just as in mastering a stick-shift car, we must have permission to make our own mistakes (what I think of as each person's *sovereign* mistakes); we must be permitted to do it badly before we can do it smoothly and well.

Aristotle said, "The best way for a student to get out of difficulty is to go through it." It's easy to see the applicability of Aristotle's thought to any process that invites meaningful learning and growth—psychotherapy, for example. When we stop avoiding a problem or lying about it to ourselves, and start to experience how it feels ("go through it"), only then can changes begin and a solution be found.

In fact, many young people these days seem to have a remarkably good sense of how important it is to embrace honest mistakes,

and this may explain why they can become disenchanted with traditional music study. Adventurous recreations like snowboarding clearly show the value of honest mistakes. It takes three days to learn to snowboard, I've been told: one day of falling down constantly (and painfully), another day to figure it out better, and by the third day you're snowboarding with style. Young people also love computers, mastering the systems quickly—almost intuitively—and yet never reading a manual. We older folks envy their fearless acceptance of computer mistakes; we sense that they've got the right idea about quick learning.

Cultural factors can also determine whether a person decides to embrace mistakes. A Korean woman was complimented on the precision and articulate fluency of her English, a language she learned as an adult. She attributed her success to the fact that she was female:

> Oh, it is much more easy for a Korean woman to learn
> than for a Korean man. She can afford to make mistakes.
> When a man makes a mistake, it is an affront to his masculine pride, to his great Koreanness. He is programmed

to feel shame. So he learns six sentences, six grammatical forms, and sticks to them. He's safe inside this little language; his pride is not wounded. But when a woman makes mistakes, everybody laughs. She's "just a girl"—she's being "cute." So she can dare things that a man wouldn't begin to try for fear of making a fool of himself. I could make a fool of myself, so it was easy for me to learn English.[4]

Suppression and denial

Whenever we play inattentively and ignore or explain away mistakes, we suppress the learning process. This can happen in various ways. There are some mistakes that never take place in practice but actually should have; they've been suppressed, which is what the traditional approach explicitly encourages. Another example of suppression is correcting a flaw so instantly and hastily that we are barely aware it ever happened; this is a form of denial—not allowing ourselves to accept reality.

> *A suppressed mistake is unfinished business.*

However we suppress a mistake, we deny the truth of the moment. A suppressed mistake is unfinished business. It's not gone; it's been swept under the rug, and it will very likely reappear at the most inopportune time—still demanding completion.

Think of suppressed emotion—as in the smiling, amiable person who is actually carrying a chronic, hidden anger. That suppressed anger is certainly not gone; in fact, it may lash out inappropriately under stress. It may also turn inward and make the person chronically ill. To suppress an emotion takes energy; it is a major internal conflict and isn't healthy.

If we make surprising mistakes onstage, it's often because we're in an altered state there—more open and vulnerable—and truth will emerge. This openness has a wonderfully positive side, when we discover unexpected spontaneity, communication and artistry in front of an audience. But a more unsettling effect can be that the customary, superficial controls we exerted in the practice room no longer seem to work. Being onstage signifies real account-ability (which is why we get nervous); the chickens come home to roost, and suppressed mistakes will surface.

There have been times onstage when I've watched in disbelief while my finger blithely played a wrong note I was sure I'd fixed months ago. But was it fixed?

Memory can be selective and unreliable. Perhaps my run-throughs weren't nearly as perfect as I thought they were—it's awfully easy to discredit seemingly minor errors, consider them unimportant when they happen, and correct them impatiently as we go, saying to ourselves, "There!—*that's* what I meant to play—I just wasn't paying attention." This split-second correction is forgotten immediately. After a while we don't perceive that such mini-corrections ever took place; the ego discounted them, but the trouble is that the body still remembers the wrong note *and* the right note as equally valid bits of information, still waiting to be sorted out. The body honestly doesn't know which is which.

For example, I may have programmed myself like this: first, play a wrong note; second, say "Oops!" (or whatever colorful one-syllable word may pop out); and third, deliberately play the right note. All in rapid succession. This same sequence happens repeatedly when that note is particularly tricky.

Is anything being corrected? Not really. What happens is that the computerlike body faithfully remembers the entire sequence (including the "Oops!"), doesn't make any judgments about it, and proudly repeats the whole thing back the next time. The body thinks that this is exactly how the piece of music goes (play a G, say "Oops," play a G-sharp).

So the mistake maddeningly reappears. Why shouldn't it? It was suppressed, not processed. "Aha!" I hear some readers exclaiming, "that's what we've been saying all along. The solution is simple— don't permit the mistake in the first place, and you'll never have to worry!" What's wrong with that idea?

This is an important question, and the answer is a physical one. To understand the flaw in the traditional reasoning we simply have to notice how it feels to avoid the mistake, what it costs us to insist on 100 percent accuracy in the practice room. Simply put, supervising our own movements so much feels unnatural. To be sure, we can always keep the music immaculate by playing *ver- rrrryyyy slllowwwlllly*, but that yields a limited result; we won't be able to handle a fast tempo, which will feel frighteningly out of control. Or we can choose a moderate tempo and steer each finger carefully to all the correct destinations, but this feels stiff and tiring, because it's asking the same muscles and nerves to do two jobs at once, namely, *find* the note and *play* the note. That won't prepare for a fast tempo either; things will probably fall apart if we try to "loosen up and be spontaneous" (as we're often exhorted to do). There will be too many notes to find, and physical tension will accumulate while accuracy breaks down. Another flaw in such overcontrolled playing is that the mind plays too central a role; we're largely relying on our thought processes to find each note. If concentration is disrupted for any reason, the notes fall apart. Playing that is held together more by willpower than real technique is fragile playing indeed.

> *Playing that is held together more by willpower than real technique is fragile playing indeed.*

The natural way, the ideal we aspire to, is just to trust ourselves and *play*, with a free flow of energy. No need to concentrate so hard on finding each note. The body itself will find the notes, because it has had an ample chance to integrate their specific locations and spatial relationships in its own physical way. But for this method to work we must first admit that the body has its own logic, its own way of sorting through things.

For example, when you learned to feed yourself as a baby, you brought the mashed peas enthusiastically to your nose or your chin as a way of mastering the location of your mouth; now you trust that mastery totally, and no concentration is required. (You might want to try it right now: pantomime the spoon-to-mouth process in the enthusiastic hit-or-miss way all babies do it, then try it as if you aren't sure where your mouth is, but imagine you've been admonished *never* to make a mistake. Compare the degree of tension in your forearm.)

Refined motor skills can become reliable, accurate, and effortless. All that's really needed is a down-to-earth understanding of programming and processing. By integrating honest mistakes, we also integrate comfort and physical freedom into the control we eventually achieve. It becomes a new sort of control altogether.

Chaos

In the pristine world of classical music, the apparent chaos of mistakes is an unsettling notion. Uneasiness about chaos has unquestionably muddled our thinking on the subject of wrong notes. We certainly aren't surprised by the chaos of mistakes in gymnastics, skiing, or our other "down-to-earth" examples. The beginning skier *expects* gross mishaps, knows they serve a purpose, and understands that they're temporary. But in classical music we cringe from the ugliness of wrong notes, hate the idea of desecrating the purity of Mozart, and—most of all—we dread public embarrassment.

But don't mistakes encourage chaos? I've often heard teachers and students ask this question, implying that chaos is something to avoid.

Interestingly, thinking in the arts can be quite conservative when compared with the sciences. Modern science has embraced chaos theory as a potent, positive, exciting interdisciplinary insight into how things work. What this theory says is that patterns which appear to be chaotic and random (such as the frequency of tornadoes or the turbulence of a mountain stream) are really evidence of an unseen "higher" system of organization.

In business training, chaos theory implies that managers should relax their ideas about controlling everything, and expect plenty of unpredictability in a company's internal and external environments en route to their long-term goals. This is considered a standard, modern outlook.

Chaos theory is an open-systems theory. Thus it takes the view that various processes in life are not self-contained but in fact affect each other in a dynamic, moment-to-moment way. Our physical well-being, for example, is an open system responding in an ongoing way to other systems (emotions, barometric pressure, external events, what we've eaten, and the like). Open-systems theories embrace the complexity, dynamism, and wholeness of life, and give up the idea that the world is predictable or that we are in control. Since open-systems views are not reductionist, they are rarely neat and clean.

Chaos theories were little accepted until fairly recent times. Aristotle, Galileo, Kepler, Descartes, Newton, and others exalted logic, rationality, order, the mechanical "watchmaker's view" of nature, and believed that in time all events would become predictable. They believed in direct cause-and-effect, in a way that is now generally considered rather simplistic.[5]

Nature, as an open system, operates on "feedback loops"— momentary information from one system that immediately affects another system, such as the interdependence of predatory animals and prey. Other examples of feedback loops: the checks and balances within democracy, economic supply and demand, a thermostat and furnace, a conversation between two people. Feedback processes are not regular and steady; rather they have moments of stillness followed by bursts of activity, in a pattern that at first glance may appear to be random.

Mastering musical performance skills is not a totally controllable or rational enterprise; it is a dynamic, natural, open-systems process. There is a mind system (my thoughts), a body system (what my muscles and nerves are experiencing), and an emotional system (my feelings), just to name a few.

The various systems are in constant flux and interact differently from one moment to the next. This is reality. When we "process a mistake" we open ourselves to information about this vital dynamic. The violinist's left hand may say, "So what if my octave leap was correct yesterday in measure 63; that may have been a fluke, and *right now* I'm not totally sure how large an octave feels in that spot. Can you give me a chance to master that interval better?" How does the left hand say this? In the only way it knows how—by landing on a specific wrong note. That mistake produces a valuable piece of information in a feedback loop.

> *Mistakes form a dynamic language of inner communication.*

Thus the body system, which is a sort of parallel system with its own logic, seeks a way to communicate with the mind-system about solving a specific problem. Mistakes, from this viewpoint, are never random. In fact, mistakes form a dynamic language of inner communication.

The open-system way of practicing is fascinating and absorbing. You never know what's going to happen next. The key is to relax, focus, and see what the systems have to tell you in any particular moment.

But in the traditional approach to practicing we shut systems down. We take a far more dreary cause-and-effect approach; we demand consistency and insist on steady, demonstrable progress. Therapist Anne Wilson Schaef sees this as a wider societal problem: "In a system that demands perfectionism, mistakes are unacceptable. We cannot learn from our mistakes, because we must pretend that we never make any. We must hide them or cover them up."[6]

It's intriguing to explore mistakes as pure evidence. In the world of science, as Briggs and Pear have put it, "Systems theory is not as gray or mechanical an idea as it sounds. In fact it can be quite lively . . . nonlinear feedback can turn the simplest activity into the complex efflorescence of a fireworks display."

The universal characteristics of systems are strikingly relevant to music practice in many ways. Mastering music is autonomous learning that involves many facets of a person. Scientists have found that the greater an organism's autonomy, the more feedback loops it needs both within itself and in its relationship to its environment. Thus, the feedback phenomenon is an essential part of true autonomy. Secondly, in a complex system, cause doesn't immediately lead to effect; there may be some delay. Think of the time it takes to integrate the technique involved in a really challenging piece of music. Consequently, students who don't trust the natural learning process just won't give it enough time to work, and they'll never discover their own capacity to play difficult, virtuosic music. And finally, systems often follow a pattern of "worse before better." Therefore changes that produce better results immediately should usually be suspect: if you "fix" the mistake the first time you repeat the passage, you may be interfering with valid feedback and short-circuiting a deeper learning process.[7]

Our training, and our schooling in general, has exalted the quick, right answer, and the sharp line between right and wrong. But the systems world to which I am alluding is a world of patterns, a nonverbal realm in which (for musicians) the body truth is the central truth. After all, music is made using the vocal mechanism, the breath or the hands—not the brain cells alone. In this wordless realm of experience, labels such as "right," "wrong," "mistake," and "correct" can be misleading. For example, say you had to jump to a B-flat, but you keep landing on an A-flat instead. That A-flat could be understood as a wrong note or as a "right-note-in-the-making," depending on your view of process.

Look back at "negative" events in your personal life: a relationship that ended badly, a job you left, a loss you felt, a struggle. After some time has gone by, do you still see these as random misfortunes that you wish had never happened, or do you see them as indispensable components of your unique journey of growth and learning? They may seem like parts of a meaningful pattern that is just now beginning to emerge. So perhaps these experiences weren't negative at all, if we take the systems view. Neither are honest mistakes.

Sometimes patterns can be truthful in a way that literal (reductionist) words cannot be. All the arts, including music, create patterns imbued with a special sort of meaning; as Isadora Duncan reportedly said, "If I could say it, I wouldn't have to dance it." Patterns are often more complex and sophisticated than our minds can grasp. H. G. Wells considered the mind a "clumsy forceps" that "crushes the truth a little when grasping it."[8]

Mindfulness

To perceive the shifting patterns of reality, to practice well in an open-systems way, is quite simple; all that's required are clear intentions, self-acceptance, and that detached, ongoing awareness of the truth of the moment that the Buddhists call mindfulness.

In selfless, mindful awareness, there is a serene sense of wholeness. Opposites such as good-bad, pleasure-pain, win-lose, right-wrong, are no longer seen as opposites at all, but as essential, interrelated components of the turning wheel of life.

Learning to swim, read, ski, whatever—the real grasp of it, the breakthrough, comes from a shift within the learner. It is a shift to mindfulness and acceptance. Something lets go (the illusion of control), the person becomes more relaxed and at the same time more observant, the process begins to be trusted, some kind of inner connection is made. This connection can't be pinned down precisely in words, and really can't be taught. This is the genuine "Aha!" To sense such authentic learning taking place within us is one of life's great fulfillments.

With a shift to mindfulness, the music practice-room—instead of teaching us boredom and defeat—can provide us with breakthrough moments of discovery, of pure process, of the wholeness of experience and the "juiciness" of learning.

4 | Step by Step
A Guide to Healthy Practicing

Good practicing, of any musical instrument or genre, is a creative process. It needn't be predictable, repetitious, or tedious. Practicing takes us on the sort of lifelong odyssey that rewards each discovery with a new set of intriguing questions. The longer we experience this odyssey, the more open to new understandings we become, and there's always something new to discover.

While the principles of healthy practicing are simple, there is real intensity too—the intensity of sustained focus. One decision after another has to be made: what to do next, in what way, and with what specific intentions. When we make decisions astutely, the payoff is solid and satisfying, the result feels right, and practicing becomes its own sweet reward, not dependent on anyone else's approval. And when breakthroughs happen, they can be surprising and exciting.

There are no universal recipes to follow, because only in each moment does a good pathway emerge, based on immediate perceptions. You try something and get a specific result, and only then do you know what to do next—go back and repeat, go forward, focus on a smaller or larger segment, or try a new strategy altogether. This flowing, nonjudgmental openness to events, this acceptance of how things really are (regardless of prior intentions), is called by Gestalt psychologists the "continuum of awareness." It's quite a refreshing and peaceful state for humans to be in, and it leads to maximum productivity as well. Finding that observant state on a daily basis may not always be easy, but it's certainly worth the effort.

My dog, for example, is supremely in touch with the moment, effortlessly living just such a continuum. Frederick Perls would say she thus demonstrates the "healthy Gestalt principle" in which "the most important unfinished situation will always emerge and can be dealt with."[1] She might be focused on eating her supper right now and on scaring off the mailman five minutes from now; in any event her momentary priorities are compellingly clear and she acts on them without hesitation. We complicated humans, however, aren't always fully awake to the moment we're in, and our focus is easily distracted and muddled. When that happens, according to Perls, "We function badly and we carry hundreds and thousands of unfinished situations with us, that always demand completion." The implication for music practice is obvious: even when the most pressing issue emerges, we may simply not be paying attention to it.

Much of the time we go along just fine, though, with good attention—until a particular event jostles us out of the continuum of awareness. This is usually something unpleasant, in most cases a mistake. Then our overactive brains start thinking, interpreting, rationalizing, avoiding, despairing, anything but holding on to our simple awareness of the here-and-now, just as it is. We take events too personally and are too anxious to justify ourselves. We go off on a tangent, thinking, "What's wrong with me? I know that note! It's easy! It wasn't a problem yesterday. I need to pay better attention." Such thoughts are a waste of time and mental energy. While we are chattering away internally, we are ignoring all the helpful, objective evidence. In Perls's apt description, "We flee into the past, expectations, good intentions, or free associations—jumping like a grasshopper from experience to experience, and none of these experiences are ever experienced, but just a kind of flash, which leaves all the available material unassimilated and unused." By charting our own practicing course every day, we keep a healthy focus on reality.

Practicing also cannot have an all-purpose recipe because each musical piece is unique and presents unique performing challenges. People are also unique in their personalities and learning strategies or preferences; some love methodical routines, some thrive on novelty and intuition, and some want rational explanations for everything. What works wonderfully for one may not be so good for another; thus there are countless effective "right" ways to practice anything, and it's not very helpful to offer doctrinaire advice.

Finally, many concepts about playing music can only be communicated physically, by demonstrating, experimenting, mimicking, feeling for signs of tension, assessing how things look. Sentences in a book can only go so far in conveying such concepts, since their essence lies in the realm of bodily experience.

Still the question arises: is it possible to produce a helpful step-by-step guide to practicing? I hope so, because I've heard many requests for an outline of what to do, a practical and detailed sequence to follow. This chapter is as close to a step-by-step guide as I can imagine.

Fundamentally, though, I offer these steps in the spirit of suggestions, open to infinite variation and adaptation. Perhaps the sequence I describe will be most useful not as a recipe but as an *example* of what one might do when practicing with freedom, honesty, and focus.

Specific musical examples will be found in chapter 5. Although some descriptions refer to specific types of instruments such as strings or the piano, the principles apply equally well to any instrument—including the voice—with little need for translation.

What is healthy practicing?

Let's define it as simply as possible. Practicing is healthy when it's:

FREE OF STRAIN, physical discomfort, tension, or fatigue
FREE OF CONFLICTS between body and mind
PRODUCTIVE—getting good results in a short time
FUN mentally and physically.

These four characteristics are crucial, since they make each moment more pleasurable and contribute to long-term achievement and satisfaction.

The approach presented here is not exotic in any way. It is not a complex system of specific new steps that need to be memorized. Rather, healthy practicing is a natural, straightforward process based on logic and simple common sense.

The components of the process are outlined in the facing table, with explanations on subsequent pages. When implementing steps that proceed in a sequence, never go through them hastily or mechanically; always wait for a sense of satisfaction with one before proceeding to the next. The time spent on each step will vary from day to day according to how you feel.

Bring the mind-body system to a practice-ready state

Don't skip this part. It's impossible to overstate the importance of this transition—the transition from our hectic round of daily activities to the calm, responsive mindfulness of practice-readiness. What we seek is an agreeable state of being that blends alertness with serenity.

Most of us find ourselves dashing around much of the time, coping with countless immediate situations, planning ahead, multitasking, never wasting a minute. But if, for example, you had made plans to meditate for half an hour during the day, you would certainly make sure to schedule several extra minutes to relax, clear your mind, and invite a special receptive mental state to take over before starting your meditation. Otherwise there would be no point in trying to meditate at all. Practicing is much the same: it could easily be thought of as a form of working meditation.

Therefore, devote five minutes or so to making a mental transition. Do this even if you're pressed for time; the first five minutes are the most important of all. Invite your mind to become calmer,

Healthy Practicing: The Process

Bring the mind-body system to a practice-ready state.

1. WARM UP in a leisurely way; awaken to your body.

2. REMIND YOURSELF what the instrument feels like.

3. REMIND YOURSELF of your general intentions for practicing.

Address the music at hand.

4. CHOOSE a section to focus on— decide exactly where you will begin and end.

5. IMAGINE in energetic detail how you want the specific passage to feel.

6. PLUNGE IN with gusto—no caution!

7. OBSERVE results closely.

8. RELAX and take a moment to digest.

9. DECIDE, on the basis of the evidence, whether to repeat the same steps, consolidate your gains, or move on to another focus.

Take a break.

10. CLEAR YOUR HEAD every twenty minutes or so by getting up and walking around for a couple of minutes. This is a highly concentrated activity, and breaks keep you refreshed in body and mind.

less scattered, more ready to focus. The best way I know to do this is to breathe deeply and become absorbed in the sensations of a simple physical warm-up, such as the routine I will describe later in this section. It doesn't really matter what the warm-up is, as long as it's extremely basic and is done in an engrossed, unhurried way.

To practice well, we must—somehow—ease the grip of our take-charge egos. This means relinquishing control (or more accurately the *illusion* of control) because that's the only way to get at the truth of how things really are. Otherwise our perceptions are tainted with self-deception and we can never tell whether we actually know something or only half-know it; we can't tell what unfinished business needs our attention. And if we don't find out the truth in practice, when will we? There's only one answer: during a performance.

> *If we don't find out the truth in practice, when will we?*

Luckily, the practice room is a workshop, not a concert hall. We're not there to make a good impression (on whom?), but to learn the piece at hand so thoroughly that it becomes genuinely secure and comfortable. In fact, there are times when good basic practicing doesn't resemble performing at all. It's an exploratory process which is frequently rambunctious, inaccurate, fragmentary, and far from pretty. Thus it's especially important to have a place to work where you can shut the door and be alone—the same way a carpenter needs a separate workshop. Practicing may be fun for us, but it's not intended to be fun for listeners.

1. WARM UP in a leisurely way; awaken to your body.

To make good music, vocally or instrumentally, involves the whole body. Limber up for a few minutes and get your blood circulating— stretch vigorously, do large arm circles, shake out your hands and arms, run in place a bit, flex your spine, and let your head dangle in different directions to loosen up the all-important neck, jaw, and shoulder regions. You want to end up feeling like an alert, energized rag-doll. As you do the physical warm-up, don't just go through your routine mechanically while thinking of other things; notice fully how every part feels to you; think in terms of questions (Do I need to loosen up my neck a bit more?). Don't forget that you are also warming up your mind by helping it become a detached, focused observer of precise bodily sensations.

2. REMIND YOURSELF what the instrument feels like.
The first notes I play every day are simple, abstract, improvised warm-ups, not industrious routines full of structure and repetition. What's important is how things feel, not whether I dutifully slog through my daily dozen. Scales and arpeggios, played at a good clip, are not warm-ups at all, but feel much more like preliminary performances. Just as athletes warm up their bodies before an event, musicians need a good leisurely getting-reacquainted-with-the-instrument warm-up before attempting any sort of measurable result, such as a scale, arpeggio, or specific exercise.

For example, with a string instrument, play some extremely long, firm tones in random patterns, savoring in a leisurely way the strength of each finger in turn on the fingerboard, the resistance of each string, the flow of the bow arm, the integration of breathing into the act of playing. Wind players can similarly use improvisatory long tones to warm up the embouchure slowly and rediscover satisfying sensations of inhaling, exhaling, and sustaining notes throughout the range. Singers can isolate different components of their singing—good posture, basic breathing, chest and head registers, various vowel formations, as well as nonmusical vocal gymnastics like growls or sighs or whistle-tones—all with a sense of curiosity and discovery, and relishing every sensation.

What we're doing is establishing something helpful: a physical point of reference. We're defining *concretely* how we want everything to feel (vividly comfortable), and this will inspire the rest of our practicing because it will give us something abundantly healthy and specific to aim for in every situation. The idea is to connect this luxuriant physical freedom with the exacting details of performance.

For pianists, who as a rule may be less likely than other musicians to indulge in relaxed, abstract warm-ups, here are some more detailed suggestions. Hold one arm about a foot above the keyboard, select one finger to land on, and drop the full weight of your arm on any white key at random. Allow yourself to miss! It doesn't matter if you do. As you hold whichever note(s) you landed on, keep the finger strong; don't let the joints cave in as the arm-weight follows through. Enjoy that firm, thorough contact with the key-bed and the big resonant tone your arm has produced. Think of *wallowing* in the note as you hold it down—releasing wrist and elbow and letting them wiggle around rag-doll style to fully establish their looseness. While you're at it, roll your head around slowly too and limber up your shoulders and spine.

When you're satisfied with that, do the same with other fingers. Then the other arm. Then mix, alternate, whatever. Try it on black keys. Take your time—be deliberately lazy about it. Keep going until you feel completely warmed up, no matter how long it takes. In fact, though, five minutes of this will probably be more than enough; relaxing and focusing make each moment amazingly productive.

For pianists, black keys are an adventure; they keep us humble on a daily basis. (Oddly, the advice books on piano technique rarely mention this basic truth). Black keys are in fact a narrow landing strip (if we dare to land on them courageously), with sloping sides that are easy to slip off of. They are, quite simply, easy to miss. Good! That's just the sort of naked truth we're interested in. When you miss one, do so with gusto, and laugh. You'll find the key sooner or later! Probably sooner, if your ego doesn't interfere. The warm-up is our opportunity to reestablish a solid physical feel for the black keys, every day.

The great cellist Pablo Casals used to say, even when he was well into his eighties, that he needed to "find" the note E-natural every morning, and then he would feel more connected to the cello and ready to play. This wonderful example of humility, self-honesty, and focus exemplifies the basic mind-set of productive practicing: assume you know nothing, and let the body be your constant source of information.

3. REMIND YOURSELF *of your general intentions for practicing.*
Here are some thoughts to get your mind ready for work. Be sure to maintain a cheerful curiosity toward the whole experiment.

- I'm a detective: what new evidence will there be today?
- All bets are off!
- I assume I know nothing and have retained nothing from yesterday.
- I'm not going to be clever in a superficial way; I've done that before and I know it usually backfires.
- I gladly relinquish control, and the practice room gives me a golden opportunity to do so.
- I willingly give up the tension of manipulating or supervising everything I do.
- Accuracy, control, refinement: these will be the *destination*, not the *starting place* of my practicing.
- I know that unexpected events—like mistakes—are full of priceless information that I can't get any other way. So I hope to flush out some juicy, honest mistakes.
- When I overdo things and take chances, I learn faster.
- By the time I leave this instrument (even if it's only ten minutes from now), I'll know that I did some honest work and made a tangible improvement in at least one identified challenge. And that will be a satisfying feeling that no one can take away from me.

Address the music at hand

This section offers a way to penetrate the surface of a piece, get right to the bone, to the unadorned truth of what needs to be learned and improved that day. Having warmed up into a limber and energized state of mind and body, we're ready now to roll up our sleeves and dissect things uncompromisingly, just like mechanics dismantling a machine in order to help it run more smoothly when it's put back together. This daily technical taking-apart serves two essential functions: *background practice*, a way of learning the music well in the first place, and then *maintenance practice*, a way of keeping it in robust shape as long as it's in our active repertoire.

Of course, we're not forgetting the ultimate purpose of it all: the beauty of musical expression. Now and then, maybe every fourth day or so, put the "machine" back together for a brief test-run. Relax and make music from the heart. If you're not ready to perform the whole piece, do a section or two. Trust the work you've done, and you will be pleasantly surprised at how effortless and responsive your technique is. And because the mechanics have become easy and "part of you," you'll find it natural to express the music in fresh, spontaneous ways. After this pleasant checking-in with the music, go right back to the constructive work of dismantling and focusing on specifics.

4. CHOOSE *a section to focus on—decide exactly where you will begin and end.*

Divide and Conquer is a general strategy that always works. No subsection of a piece is too humble to merit our curiosity and serious attention. It may be literally one note (Did I feel relaxed and confident landing on it?) or two notes (Have I truly experienced the space between them?). We build mastery by integrating all these small units.

If you're not sure where to start, select one phrase. If you're at the piano, you might start with only one hand—always a productive way to dissect the music even if you don't think you really need to.

Once you've decided you'll start *here* and stop *here*, stick to your plan, whether or not it goes well. With this clear focus and physical commitment, you will fortify your mastery if things go well and expose honest mistakes if they don't, so you win either way.

How long a passage should you choose? It's difficult to prescribe this, but if you have taken on too much, you'll know right away because the detailed physical questions won't be clearly defined and several repetitions won't yield any new understandings. When in doubt, work small—in short units. If those begin to feel too easy, you'll know right away that it's time to take on more. (But always remember to come back and work small now and then, for the purpose of maintenance.)

Another way to go about it is to start from the beginning—boldly and freely—ready to stop and work things out whenever you fumble. Let's say you miss a note in the fourth measure. Fine. That note now becomes the last note of a practice segment. Go back a few notes, enough to create some context, and repeat enough times for your hand to teach itself the distances involved. Let your body figure it out in its own way, and that may take several repetitions to happen. Even if you get it right the first time, stick to the plan to repeat the segment. The mistake you made was honest, and the correction may need a bit of time to sink in. There's always that temptation to fix things on the first try, using a little extra willpower to do so; have the wisdom to resist!

> *The idea is to* let *it happen, not* make *it happen.*

The idea is to *let* it happen, not *make* it happen. This distinction is crucial, but it may be elusive at first. We are more accustomed to supervising the outcome, measure by measure, just as we've often been told to do. Learning to trust oneself is a fascinating challenge in any field of endeavor. The amazing ease one can find is a central point in Denise McCluggage's *The Centered Skier*:

> That's one thing wrong with letting it happen—it is *ease-y*, effortless, and we do not trust the effortless way. We seem to have absorbed through our very pores the notion that there is some unnamed merit in the hard way. We credit as "real" only that which we *do on purpose*, that which takes teeth-gritting effort. We belittle or ignore that which we do without deliberate intention, that which seems to *happen*. If we cannot take credit for the doing, we discredit it.[2]

5. IMAGINE *in energetic detail how you want the specific passage to feel.* Imagining an action in detail is practically the same neurological experience as performing the action, according to research in the field. If you sit still and think intently about kicking a ball, specific nerves and muscles in the leg will energize even though the leg does not move. Somewhere I came across an interesting term for such imagining: *feelmage.* Not an image of how an action will look, but a feelmage of what the body's neuromuscular experience will be.

Giving positive imagined shape to our actions *before* we try them out is a more powerful tool than vaguely thinking, Let's just start in and see what happens. Such pre-imagining is a wonderful habit to get into, as it focuses the body and mind, dramatically affecting the quality of the phrases we actually play. It also reinforces the main focus of healthy practicing: We no longer ask only, "Was that result correct?" but far more importantly, "Did that feel really good?" These are not the same questions at all, and there can be quite a gap between the two answers we receive. Closing that gap is the goal.

For now, let your feelmage (of staccatos, jumps, articulations, legato melodies) be large, generous, emphatic—*regardless of dynamics or other subtleties in the score.* Enlarging every gesture helps your physical self to understand more quickly how everything fits together. The subtleties can eas-

> *Refining our actions is never a problem, once they make sense to the body.*

ily be dealt with later; refining our actions is never a problem, once they make sense to the body. A good strategy for pianists is to close the lid over the keyboard and pantomime a passage exuberantly on the flat wooden surface of the lid. Focus on the kinetic aspect of the music—a lively rhythmic choreography for your hands and arms.

Every piece of music—even the most gentle or slow one—is technical in some way. Every sequence of notes needs to become palpable under our fingers or in our voices, because only when we've attained technical assurance can we even attempt subtle effects like "extremely even" or *pianissimo.* Did you ever notice that inexperienced performers falter most often in the "easy" parts, not in the "hard" parts they've practiced so thoroughly? Most likely those easy parts were never totally learned, in a physical sense; that important step was never completed. Thus it's always good to know, "What's technical about this section?" so that we'll know how to practice each part more pragmatically.

Practicing "easy parts" works best when we put ourselves under a bit of pressure—deliberately—in order to bring the physical technique to the forefront. If you have a series of slow, quiet chords, speed them up and play them loudly with an almost reckless sort of freedom, and then you'll instantly know exactly where the potential weaknesses are. (And what you discover will be valid.) Practice most things ad lib, out of tempo; this also helps you focus purely on the physical, as it allows you to speed up or slow down for the sole purpose of technical self-assessment.

Thus, when you imagine the musical segment you're about to practice, you needn't picture all the aesthetic refinement of a finished performance—yet. Your image (or feelmage) at this point should be big, exaggerated, free.

6. *PLUNGE IN with gusto—no caution!*

If there is a centerpiece to my practice philosophy, it is this point. Many music students approach the music they are learning with too much deference—caution and physical timidity—as if they were afraid to mess it up, or as if they somehow felt a bit guilty in advance. They don't dare bring any real energy to it until they know better how to control and refine everything. Sadly, this attitude guarantees that they will fall short of their dreams of confident mastery.

Here again, think of tennis or basketball; we could never master those skills if we approached practice sessions in an apologetic, under-energized way. Why should music be any different?

Professional musicians infuse everything they do with a whole-body commitment of energy. Picture Ella Fitzgerald, Yo-Yo Ma, Artur Rubinstein, Bobby McFerrin, or any great performer you admire. Amateurs and students can have energy like theirs too, once they focus their intentions. Anyone can resolve to bring full energy to a piece on the very first day of practicing it, and the results will inevitably reward that courage.

Practicing should take on an athletic sort of rhythm:

Relax—Imagine—Go for it—Assess the result;
Relax—Imagine—Go for it—Assess the result.

Relaxing fully after each practice phrase gives us the chance to gather ourselves and integrate vital energy into the next phrase. And when music is played with vital energy, everything *registers*: our bodies understand and remember what is learned. Nothing feels vague. If the passage involves an obvious risk—like a big jump at the piano or a quick shift on a string instrument—land as proudly and firmly on the wrong note as you would on the right note. Never recoil from a mistake. (But do notice each one and make sure to process it patiently.)

Right or wrong, the results will be clear, and when the passage does begin to go consistently well, we will have earned our success honestly and the learning will stick. By contrast, to practice with low energy is to stay forever in a misty twilight of sort-of knowing the piece, an inconsistent, frustrating state familiar to many a music student.

7. OBSERVE results closely.

Be detached—in the best sense. Avoid the ego-driven emotional roller-coaster of "Yippee—I was great!" alternating with "Aarrggh—I messed up!" Don't take the outcomes personally. This isn't about our egos, it's about gathering objective evidence.

Observe in detail, not in general terms. There's no useful information in announcing to yourself, "I messed up that time." But there is solid information in a more specific observation: "I undershot that leap to the B-flat."

Never attribute mishaps to a lapse in concentration. That's the ego again, fantasizing that it's always in control. *If you missed the note, you don't know it.* On some level. Period! That you played it perfectly yesterday is irrelevant. Find out what the mistake is telling you today, and let every mistake be a juicy, revealing one.

8. RELAX and take a moment to digest.

Relax means let go completely. Let every part you've activated go back to neutral. If you're holding an instrument, put it down. At the piano, drop your hands to your lap for a moment (at least five seconds). Breathe and release. Let there be some silence and repose in your practicing.

Two important things are thus given a chance to happen:

- The playing mechanism—muscles and nerves throughout the body—releases any slight tension or fatigue that may have set in. It then organizes itself for the next action, rather like the reset function does on a computer.
- The physical self automatically imagines replaying the action just performed. Like a sophisticated computer, the unconscious mind sifts through the replay for information about what to do the same or differently next time. It has the marvelous innate ability to digest and process events in order to learn. Your conscious mind can't do this and isn't needed anyway.

If you allow a bit of time for this invisible process to complete itself, your next attempt is likely to be dramatically more successful. Try it and see.

9. DECIDE, *on the basis of the evidence, whether to repeat the same steps, consolidate your gains, or move on to another focus.*

Ask yourself, "Did that feel automatic, solid, and comfortable?" If the answer is yes, repeat the passage a couple more times so your body can "groove" the right action—and as you do so, continue to permit honest mistakes. Don't forget: if your body has experienced playing a passage six times wrong and once right, the problem is probably not quite corrected yet (even though you might like to think it is). The right way needs to become your dominant physical habit, which is why we need a few reinforcing repetitions.

But there's no need to overdo the repetitions. When a passage becomes a "part of you," you'll sense this and know that it's time to move on to a new learning horizon. Try a longer passage, or put two or three units together, or combine the two hands, or try a section with full musicality to see if you can trust the technique you've developed. Thanks to the thoroughness of your work to this point, you may be far more ready for a leap forward than you would have suspected.

The learning horizon is what some might call the teachable moment. In terms of risk, it means treating a given passage not too conservatively and not too wildly, but just at the edge of control (or perhaps a bit past the edge). If you have tamed that risk after a few minutes' work, you've gauged the horizon well. You might even wonder fleetingly, Why did I ever think that passage was difficult? That is a sign of excellent progress and excellent self-management.

Take a break

10. CLEAR YOUR HEAD *every twenty minutes or so by getting up and walking around for a couple of minutes. This is a highly concentrated activity, and breaks keep you refreshed in body and mind.*

Following all the steps outlined here would make it virtually impossible to develop symptoms of tension or a playing-related injury. Returning to "neutral" after each phrase, with full relaxation, means returning to a condition of zero tension. Simple mathematics dictates that adding zero to zero over and over will still result in a total of zero. In case any slight strain has accumulated for whatever reason, however, a general break every twenty minutes will allow it to dissipate. Most of us aren't used to focusing as intently, and making as many decisions one after the other, as we do when practicing well. So our minds also need—and enjoy—a total break.

To sum up

In the world of practicing, every choice we make has some effect. If we play through a piece rather idly, with nothing particular in mind, the effect is not neutral. In fact, practicing in this way can be detrimental: we lose a bit of technical security when we play things through too frequently, although this may not be obvious at the time.

In other words, if we're not actively making things better, chances are we're making them worse. Athletic coaches often tell their teams the very same thing. There's no neutral ground. That may seem harsh, but it's accurate. This explains why people so often seem to "peak" right after they've been working hard at technical mastery of a piece. As they complacently play through what they now assume they know, technical components start to deteriorate little by little from lack of the sort of maintenance we have been describing.

> There's no
> neutral ground.

Think of technical achievement as a sort of bank account. Each performance spends some money out of the account, and constructive maintenance work puts deposits back in. The steps outlined in this chapter are not preliminary; they shouldn't be jettisoned, like the booster stage of a rocket ship, once their job is done. They comprise ongoing maintenance practice, which does a beautiful job of keeping us honest and in touch with reality on a daily basis.

Keep taking the piece apart in the humble, inquisitive spirit I've described, as long as it's in your active repertoire. It will simply get better and better, in many ways. For example, tone quality—on any instrument—will naturally blossom, simply as a by-product of mind-body comfort, removal of conflict, and the unimpeded flow of energy. This is of great importance too; producing a relaxed, full, and human tone quality opens vistas of richer musical meaning for both performer and listener.

Perhaps the best reward is the most practical: *much less practice time is needed.* Honest work that penetrates directly to the issue at hand, while preserving physical enjoyment, is amazingly effective. The process I've described may seem long and painstaking, but that's only because explaining it takes a long time! Once a person is used to a detached mind-set, the approach proves to be fast and streamlined because it wastes no time. Just as in any field of learning, whenever we manage to frame the right question—clearly and honestly—we leap ahead in learning. That's when it takes five minutes to grasp what might have eluded us for five months.

This speediness is a wonderful boon to the practicer. An irony of more timid, humdrum practicing is that by the time students finally feel some mastery of the material, they've spent so many unnecessary weeks with the piece that they've begun to lose interest in it. In many cases they've also gotten bored with striving daily for a particular interpretation dictated by a teacher; any interpretation can be become stale when it is overrehearsed. But by mastering the mechanics quicker, by developing a solid basic technique that can be put to flexible use, and by keeping interpretive questions open longer, students get to spread their wings as individual, creative, spontaneous musicians. And that was the whole point of background practice in the first place.

FAQ: frequently asked questions about practicing

1. Are you saying that slow, careful practice is useless?

    Not at all. It's helpful up to a point, but usually it's not adventurous or focused enough to be strongly effective.

2. The so-called traditional approach has worked fine for me. Comments?

    a. Great! Don't change a thing.
    b. But were you really challenged by the material?

3. My teacher plays virtuosic music with ease and assurance, and believes in a perfectionistic sort of practicing. How can this be?

    Certain people are innately attuned to their bodies, and always permit their bodies to learn and problem-solve, in their own way. They may not be totally conscious of this gift because the process is so natural to them. But sometimes these same people, when in the teacher role, will still recite the conventional philosophy, which denies that same bodily wisdom. It's possible to do one thing and preach another, for any number of reasons.

4. Is it a good idea to use a metronome?

Only for short periods, as a check of tempo consistency. If we use it too much we become passive slaves to it, and our inner rhythm stays dormant.

5. If I practice a lot out of tempo, won't that encourage rhythmic inaccuracies?

Not if you understand the correct rhythm fundamentally, in your body.

6. If I stop to thoroughly "process" each mistake or weakness, won't it take an incredibly long time to learn a piece?

No, because you're getting right to the heart of the matter and you won't have to repeat the procedure over and over.

7. How can I become more aware of how my playing actually "feels"? Sometimes it seems awfully nebulous when a teacher asks me, "How did that feel?"

Warm up more thoroughly, so you have a good sense of how you want your body to feel during playing. To focus more on the physical, take away the distraction of actual notes and sounds. Try pantomime. Close the piano lid and play on that.

8. Is it worthwhile to isolate the fingers sometimes, and just work on good old-fashioned finger-independence and strength?

Absolutely.

9. What's wrong with reaching a point where you say, "Good— now I have the notes *down*"? Isn't that a nice positive reinforcement?

It's too categorical. It denies the changeability of life. It means that if you mess something up after you've declared the notes "down," you will feel more guilt than before. Keep things open and honest. Pieces do reach a point where their accuracy has become naturally consistent; the margin of error becomes so small that it's hardly noticeable.

10. Can your approach be simply stated as, "Just don't fret about wrong notes; after all nobody's perfect"?

    No. This isn't a feel-good philosophy; it's a pragmatic problem-solving plan along the road to artistry. Control, accuracy, and refinement *are* still the goals.

5 | Breakthroughs

If we are going to become dispassionate detectives in the practice room, just what sort of findings will we unearth? Will we make discoveries that can lead to real breakthroughs?

Breakthroughs, after all, are the highest objective of practicing. The enduring belief that a breakthrough can happen keeps us going day after day, and the satisfaction of a breakthrough is great indeed. When I say "breakthrough," I actually mean *transformation*—becoming a different person, in a sense; redefining oneself as capable of doing something (or understanding something) which one wasn't able to before, or finding new ease with an action that used to be a struggle. We have all had breakthroughs and know that exalted feeling. Think of learning to tie your shoes. At first you fumble with the laces and strain to remember each step of the sequence, which seems endlessly complicated and daunting. But when the body eventually digests the flow of movements in its own way, the skill that once seemed next to impossible now feels like part of you, like the easiest thing in the world, and you feel transformed—proud, newly confident, and ready for the next challenge.

The expectation of a breakthrough—a realistic expectation, in my view—is the most inspiring reason to practice. But breakthroughs won't happen when practicing is unimaginative; that sort of effort usually yields only minor, scattered improvements that don't alter one's plateau of ability.

Breakthroughs in life may seem to occur rarely and randomly, but it's exciting to think that we can invite them consciously by setting up the right conditions. This is exactly what a healthy, honest, observant body-mind dialogue can achieve. Here, then, are the sorts of findings that can lead to breakthroughs. Most pertain to technique, and the last section deals with artistry.

Spatial relationships

Sometimes good practicing is nothing more or less than target practice. Once we accept that what we're doing is fundamentally a sport, and once we stop supervising and guiding our fingers to every note, everything feels a lot riskier. It becomes clear that a new sort of learning—entirely physical—is starting to happen.

For example, at the climax of the theme in Tchaikovsky's *Variations on a Rococo Theme*—a featured musical moment—an exposed shift for the cello soloist intimidates a lot of performers (Example 1).

Example 1. Tchaikovsky, *Variations on a Rococo Theme*, op. 33, mm. 45–47.

Cellists may "nail" the shift a good percentage of the time in practice but miss it in performance, so they'd like to improve their percentage under pressure. The essential left-hand information has two components: the exact location of the high pitch that the shift lands on and the distance between the two pitches involved. How can cellists challenge and solidify their grasp of this information, which seems so abstract on the cello's fingerboard?

First, take a relaxed breath and get into the "curious detective" state of mind. If you had to find that high note from nowhere, just pull it out of the air without hesitation and play it boldly, would the pitch be accurate? Experiment by trying to do this a few times, fearlessly. Between the different tries, loosen your shoulders and take a relaxing breath; deliberately erase the slate. Chances are you will miss the note quite a few times—if not, you're probably still controlling things too much. When you do land wrong, sustain the note anyway, thinking calmly, "Hmmm, this isn't it." Notice how it feels, though. Trust your left hand to find the note more and more surely, without any anxious manipulations on your part. You'll soon see this natural improvement.

When that high note begins to feel like an old friend, turn your attention to the shift itself. Shifting is an activity of release—like tossing a ball up in one place and catching it in another; fun to do, but there's risk involved. As you start to work the shift, picture the ardent intensity the music will ultimately have in that phrase, and use that level of energy right from the beginning. Vow to hold the high note with pride, whether you land on target or three notes away. All honest information is grist for the mill, as long as you give yourself time to process it.

The great payoff is that with this attitude you simply can't lose. If you land wrong, you'll receive good clarity about whether you are undershooting or overshooting the mark; if you land right, the boldness you brought to the shift will reinforce the rightness and make the shift even more trustworthy in the future.

Each time you shift, ask your arm for spatial information about the distance. This is the most helpful "finding." Whether or not you managed to find the high note on a particular attempt may be an interesting statistic, but will that information help you find it the next time? What counts in the long run is *how* you did it, not just what the outcome was.

After a while, the shift finds a more consistent groove, and an overall spatial pattern begins to emerge and to be understood by the body—a large unity that takes in both notes and the shift between them. At this point the body registers a feeling of "Aha!"

A procedure like the one just described is an abundantly healthy way to practice something difficult, thanks to frequent relaxing, remembering to breathe, and the absence of self-interference. It's virtually impossible to develop a playing injury when you use natural motions and perform them thoroughly, without fear.

Hidden truths

Wrong notes can lead to some surprising discoveries. On the piano keyboard, an arpeggio appears to be a simple, consistent structure, the same three notes over and over (Example 2). The logical left brain thinks, Great! Just one simple pattern to learn—this ought to be easy! But as the arpeggio sweeps rapidly up and down the keyboard, we may notice some (apparently) random wrong notes. What's going on?

Example 2. Arpeggio.

As always, the first step is to relax and observe the outcome in detail. Students often find this difficult to do. Typically, after a less-than-perfect arpeggio they'll grimace and say, "That was terrible!" to cover their wounded pride. But this is just an ego-statement and doesn't shed any light on the situation. It also errs by treating the entire arpeggio as one thing—an "it"—whereas any passage actually consists of a great many individual experiences.

When we do succeed in bringing better focus to the arpeggio, we often find that for some reason the fingers tend to miss notes repeatedly in the same zone—let's say the second-to-top octave, as marked by the Xs in Example 3.

Example 3. Arpeggio with wrong notes.

What's the hand trying to communicate through the wrong notes? That the player needs to concentrate harder or just slow down? Not really. The hand is saying, "Something feels different at this spot." But if the notes are in exactly the same formation, what could be different?

Sit at the middle of the keyboard and look at the black keys right in front of you. Notice how widely they are spaced. Now glance to the far ends of the keyboard and notice the black-key spacing. Visual foreshortening makes those keys look closer together. Now place your hand on a chord right in front of you, then on the same chord three octaves away. The intervals *feel* quite different too, because the hand is now in a totally different spatial relationship to the torso, and the angle of the wrist has adjusted. We're discovering that the physical situation is not constant but ever-changing.

Now we have a cognitive clash: the logical left brain says that each octave of an arpeggio is the *same* (the notes), while the experiential right brain says that each octave is *different* (the spatial relationships).

Which perception should we believe? Clearly the right brain must prevail since it is the voice of real experience. A new question now frames our practice: if there are physical differences from one octave to the next, how much can we discover about those fascinating differences? Thus we trade in our prior frustration for a positive new attitude based on curiosity.

Eloise Ristad used an effective word for this mind-set: *tracking.* This word describes the problem-solving process accurately, which helps the verbal and the nonverbal minds to understand each other and work together. The formula goes like this:

PROBLEM: I keep messing up this passage.

STRATEGY: Don't try to fix it; play it again and *track* exactly where the problem starts.

PROBLEM: This figure feels so awkward.

STRATEGY: Don't try to fix it; play it again and *track* exactly what part of your body feels tense and when. Learn all you can about the details of this so-called awkwardness.

As you might guess, problems can evaporate magically when we shift our attitude to tracking instead of conquering. That arm just refuses to tense up when you give it permission to "talk" to you frankly, without fear of censorship or reprisal.

Einstein comes to mind once more as we delve into the mysteries of the arpeggio. Arpeggios illustrate a Musical Theory of Relativity: *things are not always what they seem.* In the abstract, time and space are constants, and arpeggios are all the same. But in the realm of experience, time and space can bend—and apparently arpeggios can bend too. The "chaos" of honest practice gives us inklings of a new (perhaps more sophisticated) kind of order.

> The "chaos" of honest practice gives us inklings of a new kind of order.

Alike but different

Luckily, the body has a knack for learning musical skills readily. But as musicians generally discover, the body also gets confused all too easily. Subtle differences between similar passages are the usual causes of confusion. And similar passages abound, since formal structure, in many musical styles, comes from the repetition or development of material, or from returning to material after wandering elsewhere. Because themes recur and play multiple roles in the architecture of a piece, numerous passages resemble each other closely, but they are also somewhat different. Themes may reappear in a new key, or with a slightly altered accompaniment, or with the notes rearranged.

After a bit of study, the mind can usually summarize these differences quite well, but the body's perceptions are different; it finds even the most minute changes hugely significant and potentially confusing. For example, putting a theme into another key often changes completely the feeling of how the notes lie on the geography of the keyboard. The great potential for confusion, often manifested by the mixing up of two all-too-similar passages, is easy to understand when we keep in mind how strongly programmable we are. Frequently these passages start exactly alike, yet they have different ways of finishing. However, *both* note-patterns have been learned, and reinforced, through repetitious practice. Can the body sort them out? This poses one of the greatest challenges to the brain and nervous system: not to mix up two well-established memory tapes—because, in a sense, both versions are right!

For example, in Mozart's Piano Sonata in B-flat major, K. 333, we have similar patterns just a few measures apart, as shown in Examples 4 and 5.

In the course of practicing we may not always notice every such parallelism in the music—we're only human, after all. But the muscles remember unfinished business and will make the necessary

Example 4. Mozart, Piano Sonata in B-flat major, K. 333, mm. 50–52.

Example 5. Mozart, Piano Sonata in B-flat major, K. 333, mm. 54–56.

mistakes to get the mind's attention. "Now why are my fingers getting confused there? Oh, I see—this passage is almost the same as that other one; I just never understood the exact discrepancies before."

Physiology

The cause of a specific insecurity can be physical. For example, the ring finger (fourth finger for pianists) is much less mobile than the others, because it is physiologically yoked to the surrounding fingers. To demonstrate the truth of this: Rest your hand on a table; open the hand and straighten out the fingers; place all the fingertips (fleshy part) on the table-top; fold the third finger under so that the entire second joint is pressed flat on the table; keeping the hand still, try to lift fingers 1, 2, 4, and 5 in turn. Three of them will lift easily, but the fourth feels paralyzed. Now try the same experiment folding only the fifth finger under.

The fourth finger is naturally weak, almost vestigial, a structural fact we contend with every day at the piano. Lots of pianists have banged away lustily on Hanon finger exercises for years, using arm and wrist muscles to help make a big noise on every note and

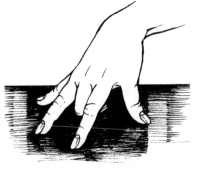 

Folding the third finger under   Folding the fifth finger under

convincing themselves in the process that evenness and power were being achieved. But this type of practice doesn't acknowledge the anatomical truth that human fingers are not created equal. Until we feel clearly the dependence and weakness of the fourth finger, how can we focus on it beneficially? We must isolate weaknesses if we want to convert them to strengths. Follow the advice that management trainees are often given in business courses: expose the problem!

Perhaps, like me, you've had some quite "logical" fingerings crumple under pressure simply because the fourth finger gave out. Given the choice, the fourth finger would usually rather *not* play the piano! Under stress, the fourth finger often behaves like a horse that refuses to go over a jump. But once we realize what's happening, we can deal with it. When our detective work reveals that the fourth finger is the culprit, it can be singled out and lingered over in practicing, with excellent results—greater confidence and reliability.

Negative space

Sometimes it's not the notes that need attention, it's the physical spaces in between. Recognizing this can lead to a breakthrough.

Imagine that you're holding a beautifully embroidered cloth. On the "right side" the details of the image are precise. Flip the cloth over and the zigzagging lines of thread appear random and chaotic.

But this isn't really chaos, as we know; it's simply a negative space—how the thread got from one stitch to the next. Both sides of the cloth are essential to the aesthetically polished result.

Many books on creative thinking offer an image like that shown here, to demonstrate that the mind simply can't decide how to interpret the image—am I seeing a goblet, or am I seeing two profiles? When you see one image, the other recedes and becomes the negative space.

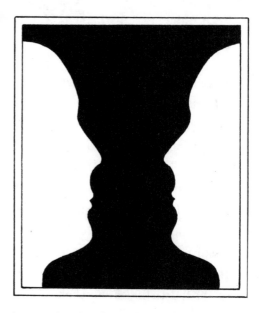

Background or foreground: a goblet or two profiles?

Take an art class, and you will find that the secret of drawing well is seeing well, which means seeing everything with an open mind, including—especially—negative space. Art instructor Betty Edwards, in *Drawing on the Right Side of the Brain*, makes the point that our drawings are often clumsy because when we try to draw separate objects—a hand, a table, a tree—we ignore the background, an area with a shape all its own. So our drawings end up cartoonlike, since cartoons present figures with little or no background. To see the image more fully is to become intrigued by negative space. Edwards's book documents astonishing breakthroughs in drawing ability when amateur artists learn to see in this new, inclusive way.

The problem with drawing familiar objects, says Edwards, is that we "know too much about them"—that all four legs of a chair are the same length, for example.[1] This conventional information may be contradicted by what we actually see, especially if the chair is viewed from an odd angle and the leg lengths appear unequal. Here again, fixed ideas interfere with truthful perception.

Similarly, musical notes are objects, and we know too much about them too—exactly where they should be and how they're supposed to sound, for instance. Adopting the method Edwards suggests, an enlightened practicer would take a more open, inclusive view, and would set out to learn the specific physicality of the notes and the spaces between them. To put it another way, what we learn in the practice room should be 50 percent notes and 50 percent negative space.

Take the familiar Chopin Nocturne in E-flat major, for instance (Example 6). The music is so lovely and pure that students are often jarred by any wrong note. As a result they tend to play it rather cautiously. The left hand, however, faces some down-to-earth challenges because it must jump around constantly, and jumps are risky. In addition, the chord-shapes change all the time, and there are lots of black keys (which are also risky).

Example 6. Chopin, Nocturne in E-flat major, op. 9, no. 2, beginning.

But if we feel guilty about the inevitable clunkers, and react by slowing down in order to be more careful and accurate, we learn very little. In fact, caution will heighten the childish, cartoonlike aspect of our playing. Different elements will stand out as distinctly as cartoon images: "Here's *this* bass note, then *this* chord over here, then this *next* chord." All will be played in a halting way because the performer has no concrete sense of the spaces between. Playing can't have lyricism, sweep, spontaneity, subtlety, or tonal beauty when there's no trust of negative space. One's muscles are simply too tight and self-conscious to join the musical flow.

The negative space of the left-hand part might be represented by the arrows in Example 7. They also represent the natural arcs inscribed in the air by the left arm as it moves from place to place—the palpable negative spaces with which we need to become familiar.

Example 7. Negative space in Chopin's Nocturne in E-flat major, op. 9, no. 2, beginning.

How can practicing improve the sense of negative space? Relax, play rather loudly (and comfortably), and vary the rhythm so the hand will land decisively in different spots. Do it freely, almost recklessly, however it sounds. Example 8 suggests two possible variations. Notice and enjoy the feel of the negative spaces—those arcs linking the notes and chords. As always, stop and process all mistakes as they occur. What we're accelerating here is the process of flushing out specific insecurities and then solidifying a new sense of mastery.

Such practicing is definitely not pretty; it's stop-and-start, it's too loud, it abounds in wrong notes (during the process), a

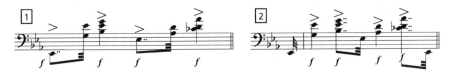

Example 8. Practice technique: rhythmic variations.

far cry from the pristine reverie of Chopin's Nocturne. This is definitely not pleasant background music for a living room; one really needs a separate practice room to work this way. In fact, the reason so many of us lose our bearings about practicing early in life is that we practice in living rooms with other family members in earshot—and healthy practice would simply sound too obnoxious, intrusive, repetitious, and unmusical for others to hear without annoyance. But it does feel good when we go about it right. In fact, most of us would practice correctly *just by instinct* if we weren't in living rooms. The body appreciates how productive this robust approach is, how little time is being wasted. The process is engrossing and fun. This sort of practice is the necessary chaos, the flip side of the refined "embroidery" of classical music.

After a few days, try once more for the subtle result—the floating, controlled *pianissimo*. Now it seems easy. The notes almost play themselves, without strain. Since the body trusts the passage and has experienced it fully, playing has become effortless.

In the realm of science as well, negative space plays a crucial role. Intellectual negative space needs to be explored in order to have a full, satisfying result. Nobel Prize—winning physicist Richard Feynman said that the true research breakthrough comes from including everything the findings are *not*—a kind of "utter honesty" in the interest of integrity. A convincing presentation of a new finding should include every logical objection, every theory that might invalidate it, all evidence that casts doubt upon it, every idea that was rejected in the process, and why.[2]

Chapter 5

Artistry

Of course the most fulfilling breakthroughs of all come when the artist within each person soars and makes new discoveries. Metaphorically, the artistic process is very much the same as the technical one: instead of gripping something, we let it go, trust the process, and trust our inner selves.

Legendary English actor Sir Alec Guinness desperately needed an artistic breakthrough as a young actor on tour, and a fellow actor, seasoned veteran Dame Edith Evans, told him exactly how to go about it. Her advice could apply just as easily to any musician.

As Sir Alec tells the story, he was asked on short notice to take over the small, comic part of a butler, and he eagerly seized the opportunity. The part gave him an excellent chance to make an impact, a "sure-fire laugh on an exit line," and at his debut performance he got not only the big laugh but a hearty round of applause as well. Feeling quite smug, he looked forward confidently to a similar victory the next night. But this time there was no laugh and certainly no applause, and thus it remained night after night thereafter. Backstage, Dame Edith feigned indifference but finally beckoned to the despairing young actor. She whispered,

> "You've lost that laugh." "What am I doing wrong?" I whispered back. "You're trying too hard. You didn't know how you got it in the first place. But it is natural to you, one day you will find it again. Take it lightly. Forget about it. But *when* it comes back make a note of what you were feeling *inside*." I thanked her and turned away, but she called me back again. "It will take about a week before you find it," she said, in a very practical way, "and once it is there you will never lose it." She was dead right. A week later the laugh was there once more; I was happy again, relaxed and, strangely, not overexcited. Edith appeared not to see me but gazed moonily at the other actors onstage.

112

What the lesson was she had taught me I am not quite
sure—some inner mystery—and yet it *was* a lesson and
I have to remind myself of it frequently.[3]

Again the performer is gently reminded to stop trying to control the outcome, but to stay flexible and focus instead on how the moment actually feels.

Alec Guinness's learning all took place onstage in front of an audience, so for him to give up control must have taken considerable courage. His succinct observations are right on target:

- The understanding he reached was tacit, unnamable, irreducible, "some inner mystery." It certainly wasn't a formula that could be repeated or stated in words.
- The learning process was fundamentally so natural that when he achieved the goal, he wasn't elated but instead felt "relaxed and, strangely, not overexcited."
- As a first step he had to acknowledge his ego-attachment to applause and approval ("quite nauseatingly pleased with myself") and let that go. In its place he developed a more alert, autonomous, and ego-less state of mind.
- Thanks to Dame Edith's words, the futility of trying to control everything is made clear: "You didn't know how you got it in the first place."

Any musician can relate to Guinness's story. How many times do we play a new passage surprisingly well the first time we try it—when there are absolutely no expectations of success? We may feel rather self-satisfied, proud of our quickness. But then, when we set out to master the passage by practicing conscientiously, the notes seem to rebel and everything becomes a struggle. It can be quite baffling.

I appreciate the way Dame Edith, despite her greater age and experience, communicated to the young actor that he had his own best answers within. She showed respect for him by giving him candid feedback ("You've lost that laugh"), not trying to fix the problem for him and refusing to take any credit for his ultimate triumph. (Maybe it helped that their relationship was not in fact a teacher-student one.) She also knew that finding solid technique involves an inner journey that takes time, and she remembered to mention this to young Alec. This helped him give himself permission to trust the process and to live through his necessary mistakes en route to the confidence he eventually found.

A related story from my own work: a few years ago I was preparing to perform the French Suite No. 3 in B minor by J. S. Bach. It contains a minuet that begins as we see in Example 9.

Example 9. J. S. Bach, Minuet from French Suite No. 3, beginning.

After becoming familiar with the notes, I began to experiment freely with the interpretation, taking full advantage of the scarcity of interpretive markings typical of Bach and other composers of his time. Since the Minuet is in minor, it occurred to me to play more slowly than usual, with a subdued hint of tragedy underlying the lilting dance. Ah—excellent! I thought as I played it, so I picked up the pencil, scribbled "melancholy" in the score, and felt quite creative and exhilarated.

The next day I looked forward to returning to the Minuet, but after I launched into it with a conscious air of sadness, I began to think, How phony and contrived! and didn't like the idea at all. Out came the eraser; no more "melancholy" in my score. A few more experiments, and I found that I now loved the Minuet played in a perky, playful, lively way, so I wrote "jaunty" in the score. The next day I tried it the jaunty way and thought, How cheap!, and out came the eraser. At this point I had to laugh, because it was clear what was happening. Any idea can be creative and beautiful when it's pure, that is, at the moment it comes to us unbidden. But if we grasp it too tightly, fix it too early, make it our rigid plan, give it a name, it can become fake and untruthful. In the case of my Minuet, the first "melancholy" idea was still artistic and could still communicate with freshness in performance; the only thing I did wrong was to define it and clutch at it a little too much.

The lessons of this story? Trust the source of inspiration. Trust ourselves more. Always leave something open to the moment. Trust that there are plenty more good ideas where the first one came from.

A Hollywood movie that deals beautifully with the question of artistic self-trust, and the artistic breakthrough, is *The Karate Kid*. The plot deals with a California teenager, Daniel, and the meaningful lessons about karate and life that he learns from Mr. Miyagi, a Japanese handyman. As in the case of Alec Guinness, the teacher is not an officially designated teacher at all.

There is a memorable scene in *The Karate Kid* which in fact has nothing to do with karate. Mr. Miyagi is absorbed in trimming a delicate miniature bonsai tree. Daniel drops in to see him, and is mesmerized by what he sees.

DANIEL: These are really beautiful!

MIYAGI: Come, you try!

D: But I don't know how to do this stuff!

M: Sit down—

D: (agitatedly) I may mess it up—I don't want to mess it up!

M: (quietly, hypnotically) Close eye . . . trust . . . concentrate . . . think *only* tree . . . make perfect picture, down

to last pine-needle . . . wipe mind clean, everything but tree . . . Nothing exist, whole world . . . just . . . tree—
   (A minute passes.)

M: You got it? Open eye . . . Remember picture?

D: Yeah.

M: (handing him scissors) Make like picture.

D: (stares at tree, hesitates)

M: Just trust picture.

D: (still staring) But how do I know if my picture is the *right one?*

M: If come from inside you, *always right one!*[4]

Daniel dreads "messing it up" and is seeking outside authority to tell him what to do. But wise Mr. Miyagi knows better and helps Daniel focus on the object outside of himself and release his ego and thus his fear. He awakens in Daniel a flow of artistic awareness. His message seems to be, "I believe in your inner sense of rightness."

6 | *Is It Good to Be a Good Student?*

Cleaning out the garage one day, I came across a dusty carton of my college notebooks from many years before. One of them was labeled Advanced Calculus, a course in which I had managed to get an A, not just once, but for two semesters. But as I paged through, I had the odd experience of gazing at notations that made absolutely no sense to me, although they were clearly in my own handwriting. In fact I had no memory at all of having written all those symbols, graphs, and equations. The truth is I had never understood a single thing about calculus then, and I certainly don't now. But one thing I had understood quite well was how to play the education game, how to be a "good student." (I introduce that term in quotes because I'm referring to someone who knows how to get an A, not someone who genuinely knows how to learn.)

Calculus was a required course, and as a music major I had no interest in learning anything from it. All I wanted was the grade. So I did what so many good students do: observe the teacher closely, figure out what he wanted, memorize some formulas and surface operations (without questioning the reasons behind them), learn to recognize which situations called for which procedures, and plug those in at the right moment.

I did get the desired grade, but I also paid a hidden price, which I only came to realize later. Those grades of A didn't give me much satisfaction, only a sense of relief that I'd gotten away with it and hadn't been unmasked as the impostor I knew myself to be. The trouble is, it doesn't feel comfortable to be an impostor; it leads to cynicism about the system (how could they have fallen for it?) and guilt. And in my case, pretending about math had become such a habit that a glum belief set in: the lifelong certainty that I had no ability to understand higher mathematics.

Now, whenever I hear myself state, "Oh, I'm no good at math," I wonder—is that really so, or is it just something I've come to believe? As a music teacher, would I accept it at face value if somebody said, "I'm no good at music"? Probably not. I'd probably think that person just hadn't had the right musical experiences.

It does give me a bit of consolation to know that even the elite math students at MIT didn't always "get it" either. They had mastered plenty of techniques and stored lots of information, but their inner grasp was only partial. According to physicist Richard Feynman:

> I often liked to play tricks on people when I was at MIT. One time, in mechanical drawing class, some joker picked up a French curve (a piece of plastic for drawing smooth curves—a curly, funny-looking thing) and said, "I wonder if the curves on this thing have some special formula?"
>
> I thought for a moment and said, "Sure they do. The curves are very special curves. Lemme show ya," and I picked up my French curve and began to turn it slowly. "The French curve is made so that at the lowest point on each curve, no matter how you turn it, the tangent is horizontal."
>
> All the guys in the class were holding their French curve up at different angles, holding their pencil up to it at the lowest point and laying it along, and discovering that, sure enough, the tangent is horizontal. They were all excited by this "discovery"—even though they had already gone through a certain amount of calculus and had already "learned" that the derivative (tangent) of the minimum (lowest point) of any curve is zero (horizontal). They didn't put two and two together. They didn't even know what they "knew."

I don't know what's the matter with people: they don't learn by understanding; they learn by some other way—by rote or something. Their knowledge is so fragile![1]

Music learning can be fragile too. Music and mathematics are alike in that students haven't totally digested a new concept until a visualization, or a palpable sense of spatial relationships, clicks into place. Then we have the classic "Aha!" moment. The surface operations have no relevance without this felt sense, this bodily experience of rightness. And it takes a bit of extra time to allow for that feeling to happen; it won't come from quick, memorized answers, which tend to be shallow responses.

> *The surface operations have no relevance without this bodily experience of rightness.*

Feynman's description of true learning mirrors that of actor Alec Guinness (chapter 5): it isn't so much about surface techniques, rather it is "some inner mystery" which is nonetheless experienced in a tangible way. I would guess that everyone longs for true learning, but external situations—especially educational settings—can lead us astray by rewarding us for pleasing others, for playing the good-student game.

The good-student syndrome

Good-student knowledge is fragile because it's incomplete. It depends on external validation. It emphasizes quickness and cleverness. Most importantly, good students are focused not on their own inner questions but on the teacher and the teacher's specific expectations. They defer to authority. In educational circles this has been termed "system dependence," the belief that if you do exactly what you are supposed to do, the system will always reward you. But educational systems don't reflect the richness—or the unpredictability—of real life.

Here again, the film *The Karate Kid* dramatizes a compelling educational point. Daniel, the young student, has now embarked on karate lessons with Mr. Miyagi, and the goal is clearly defined: to win the upcoming karate tournament against some high-school bullies who have been beating Daniel up on a regular basis. The bullies have agreed to leave him alone if he can win the tournament—something they consider highly unlikely, since they have aggressive training in karate and Daniel has none. Handyman Mr. Miyagi, although not a certified karate teacher, agrees to help Daniel prepare. He uses his ramshackle front yard as a teaching studio, so the lessons have an unconventional, almost subversive, feel about them from the start.

Daniel is willing to work hard—which stands to reason, since he's in danger of being beaten up in the match—and wants to be told exactly what to do. He needs fast results because of the stringent deadline: the date of the tournament. Lesson after lesson goes by, but Miyagi won't answer Daniel's pressing questions about how to kick or how to punch, much to Daniel's (and the movie audience's) puzzlement. Good-student quick learning is apparently being dismantled by the screenwriter, and we wonder what will take its place.

Instead, Miyagi seems to ignore karate altogether, and makes Daniel wax cars for hours on end, but with a particularly focused, circular arm movement. Day after day, all Daniel hears is "Wax on, wax off!" He is also instructed to breathe in a vigorous, conscious pattern in coordination with the waxing gestures. After waxing the cars, he must whitewash a fence (up and down, whole arm, flexible wrist), paint a house (side-to-side), and sand a deck (large circles). All these simple motions, natural to the body and thus intrinsically powerful, are not really new, but they are being activated and brought into consciousness. Since an action like sanding a floor calls for no real accuracy, it frees a person to enjoy the vigorous motion and to integrate that motion with healthy breathing as well.

But Daniel, understandably, smolders with resentment. Despite his hard work he thinks he has learned nothing, has nothing to show for his efforts. So he confronts Miyagi angrily, to which Miyagi replies with a sudden flurry of fierce karate blows from every direction (while shouting "Wax on!" or "Paint house!"). Daniel discovers to his astonishment that the waxing and painting motions are in fact perfect blocking moves. Without having tried consciously to perfect their accuracy and without being subjected to teacherly critiques on a weekly basis, he has absorbed the moves so thoroughly that they are now swift, sure, and precise. They adjust themselves instinctively to each new situation, as if Daniel had been refining these skills for years.

So he learns not only skill, but trust in his body's wisdom and in his new-found ability to improvise. This is the turning point of the movie. In the final tournament scene, Daniel's satisfying come-from-behind victory derives not from physical power or conventional strategy but from his balance, centeredness, and self-trust. He finds fresh creativity under pressure, and he and Miyagi are equally surprised at the high level of originality and skill he demonstrates in the moment of truth.

This story brings to light one of the most misleading notions about learning: that progress should always be visible and steady. We tend to expect the straight-line steady climb, especially from someone who is known to be a good student, whereas a more true-to-life pattern has plateaus and breakthroughs.

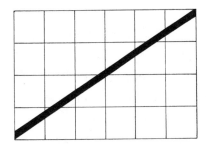
Steady climb

Plateaus and breakthroughs

It's natural to experience the alternation of plateaus with unforeseen bursts of progress. Clearly, such a pattern is not only unpredictable but will vary drastically from person to person. Progress is often invisible and hard to gauge. It takes great trust in individuals and in the learning process to accept this pattern and to resist the temptation to engineer shallow (but demonstrable) "progress."

Part of the problem has to do with self-image. Once formed, the idea of oneself as a good student is a strongly appealing one—constantly reinforced by society and difficult to let go of, even when it directly hampers a person's growth. I base this observation on many students I have known and also on my own history as a musician. Once we're identified

> *Outside approval can thus turn out to be a form of dependency.*

as good students we have a lot to lose by experimenting with new approaches. Outside approval can thus turn out to be a form of dependency and a hindrance.

My own pathway to music was complicated by this factor. Until I was seventeen, the one career possibility I had categorically rejected was that of concert pianist. This seems odd to me now, since music and piano-playing had come easily to me, I loved them both, and I also loved to perform. But school-learning had come easily too, largely because I was almost too good at the student game, alert to teachers and able to sense exactly what they wanted. The payoff at school was warm and substantial: the report card, the reputation, beaming parent-teacher conferences, and a constant message from the environment that high grades signified real self-worth. What this meant, of course, was that I had much to lose.

I would often say at the time that concert performing didn't interest me—I'd claim it was too boring, too elitist, or whatever. What I really meant was that it scared me, although I wouldn't have admitted that to myself. I was used to ease, not struggle and perseverance. What if I struggled and didn't succeed? I wasn't at all sure I could handle the inescapable accountability at the core of concert performing.

What changed this attitude was the intervention of some of my music professors in college. What they did, in essence, was call my bluff. They perceived that in pianistic terms I was a smooth faker who had avoided real challenges, and they simply told me so (in kindly words). They were surprisingly neutral, not recommending what I ought to do or not do from that point on; their helpful role in my life was simply to hold up a mirror so that I could see myself realistically. This caused me to think much harder about what I actually wanted. I proceeded to find a good teacher, the late Leopold Mittman, with whom I could begin to study the instrument "for real."

Mittman encouraged me to feel and enjoy every move at the piano. He discouraged over-intellectualizing. I learned that quick learning was irrelevant, that it takes time to gain refinement and control with any piece of music. He introduced me to the importance of physical commitment to the keyboard as a whole and to every note, having correctly assessed my general situation with the words, "You have natural facility, but no technique." He helped me find the courage to expose my weaknesses. I began tackling big pieces for the first time, using my whole body, taking new chances, enjoying the adventure of it. "Here's a virtuoso piece," he would say, slapping me on the back encouragingly, "just throw yourself at it—you'll figure it out in your own way!"

I was also learning to be honest about mistakes—letting them stand without any concealment—and learning how to process them wholesomely, without retreating from this healthy new-found exuberance of playing. Practicing became intriguing and fun for the first time. I learned to be realistic and to take my time. The mind-set in Mittman's studio was: roll up your sleeves, plunge in— who knows what you'll find today?

I remember thinking of this new approach as "practicing stupidly," since it was the exact opposite of the surface cleverness and quick results that had long been my habit. Now, even after playing a passage quite correctly, I would stop and wonder, Do I *really* get it? Often the answer was no. Such inner honesty was brand new, and I found it refreshing. Mittman explained, rightly, that I wouldn't need to practice long hours, since this "stupid" way was in fact a highly efficient way to penetrate to the bone, to what I really needed to know.

The good student in the music studio

Many an academic whiz has encountered humbling frustration in the study of music performance. Among the most common problems are shaky memory, technical limitations caused by body tension, and overcautious interpretations. Baffled and discouraged, some quit their lessons. It's difficult to accept that one's diligent efforts, so predictably crowned with laurels in school, would have such unpredictable outcomes in the musical sphere. It would help tremendously if book-smart people thought of music more as a sport and less as an intellectual activity, but this is often not the case. And for the academic perfectionist, the public nature of music-performance failures can be particularly humiliating.

But many others don't give up, and continue to seek musical wholeness—sensing that its challenges and benefits are unique and profound. Artistic self-expression is a rich reward, to be sure. But also, music mastery means self-mastery, both physical and psychological. In music, the good student comes to understand the difference between cleverness and true understanding, and learns to choose accordingly. Some people have the facile gift of quickness and thus have shortcuts available to them which other people might not have, but music performance, a great equalizer, will expose the shallowness of those shortcuts in the moment of truth. This gives clever students a precious opportunity to grow in self-knowledge through music.

ROBERTA

"Roberta," in her early thirties when I worked with her many years ago, was intelligent, level-headed, and interested in redefining her basic relationship with the piano. This took emotional fortitude, since it's not easy to confront long-established patterns that have served a self-protective purpose, even though they may in fact have been self-defeating in another way.

As a child, Roberta had always found sight-reading a breeze, and—as usually happens—she was much praised for this remarkable trait. She had a natural intellectual ability to learn complicated music quite quickly, in a rather intellectual way, and she enjoyed tackling such projects. Soon she became her teacher's prize pupil.

Unfortunately, her physical knack for playing was not precocious, so it lagged behind her mental brilliance. But the teacher wasn't troubled by this and didn't perceive that a fundamental dislocation was being set in place. On the contrary, the teacher was delighted to have such an unusually bright, responsive, and reliable student.

By the time I met her, Roberta played with clumsy but determined fingers. She gravitated to long pieces of great complexity. As she played, the music sounded impersonal and her face was locked in a fixed, pleasant smile. That smile bore no relation to the ever-changing, passionate emotions in the music. Her industrious hands seemed bizarrely disconnected from Roberta's feelings and the rest of her body. This would be evident at the end of an emphatic phrase, for example, which she could never release with a direct, convincing gesture that would signify, There!—that's *just* what I meant to say. Instead, she seemed to be going through mechanical motions.

To put it bluntly, her playing elicited no response from anyone, including Roberta herself. How did this disconnection come about?

As she eventually related it to me, her childhood pattern was that she would do anything necessary to make the pieces work, to *seem* to have enough technique to play complex music. But this often meant forcing things, contorting her young fingers; she had to "drag the technique along, battle it all the time." In lessons she would do her best to conceal this struggle. In time she developed an adversarial feeling toward her own hands ("contempt" was her word) and toward the keyboard. It is hardly surprising that she forced things, since her technical limitations might cut off the pipeline of praise and acceptance that she'd come to rely on.

Self-contempt in any form is toxic. In this tainted atmosphere Roberta's honest musical soul did not feel safe emerging. What did feel safe was to continue playing ever-harder pieces in a detached way. Their obvious difficulty worked well to keep criticism (including self-criticism) at bay. But deep down, said Roberta, "I always knew what I was lacking." She received compliments with cynical disdain, and felt "two-faced." Uncomfortable with such inner conflicts, she wondered if she would simply have to quit the piano for good.

After a break of several years, however, she took up the instrument again, as an older-than-usual college student. Something within her demanded resolution of the conflict and perceived its importance. As her teacher I sensed that the last thing she needed at this point was more detailed advice, and neither of us wanted her to feel dependent on my approval. What she did need was some way to remove her pervasive sense of shame, stemming from her old habit of faking everything. We needed to find a way to "reunite" her with her own hands and therefore with her spontaneous expressivity. And the final step would be to extend that expressivity to an audience without fear.

We approached this experimentally, with lots of activity away from the piano, such as body-movement games and dramatic improvisations (as playful as possible). We also tried isolating moments at the keyboard to an almost ridiculous extent: for example, holding one chord for a long time, sinking into it luxuriantly while exploring the question "How does this feel?" until a convincing answer came forth, a full registering of the experience of the moment, a physical sense of "Aha!" That may sound mystical, but it isn't really. The difference between shallow and full knowing at the keyboard is quite unmistakable, and one can literally see the change in students when they make this important mind-body connection.

After a while Roberta was able to reclaim the most basic technical skill of all: awareness, and enjoyment, of how things actually feel. As she put it, such a renaissance depends on restoring a basic belief, the "belief that it can be yours."

I admire Roberta's tenacity, honesty, and insight. Our dialogue went beyond music too; a divorced single parent, she was working with a psychotherapist during the time she studied with me. One focus of her therapy was to let herself be authentic, without self-judgment or blame, at all times—as opposed to presenting the smiling, controlled façade of the person she guessed others wanted her to be. Many a time during our sessions she would throw back her head with a hearty laugh, because what we were doing was "exactly like therapy." Indeed, not only did piano study often mirror psychotherapy (or the other way around), but I believed the two pursuits were intertwined. Piano-playing and psychotherapy enriched each other through shared insights and through the practical, physical, and expressive application (at the piano) of the issues at hand.

HELGA

Sometimes good students admire a teacher too much. At the time I heard "Helga" give a guest solo piano recital at my university, she was in her mid-forties and a professional artist-teacher at a major European conservatory. Expecting to enjoy the recital, I was nonplussed to hear instead an unpoetic hour of thudding, flat, ugly sounds, and I knew it wasn't the piano's fault, since this was a sweet-toned instrument from which I had heard many others elicit beautiful tones. What made it odder was that Helga consistently made unusual, deliberate-looking playing gestures, most notably a peculiar, studied way of flinging her upper arms heavily at the keyboard. Every time she did this, a particularly jarring sound resulted. What was going on—couldn't she hear what was happening?

Intrigued, I sought her out at the reception and struck up a conversation. Whenever I asked questions about her own life and career, she would deflect them and eagerly change the subject to her teacher, a world-famous pianist. Helga apparently felt that she owed everything to this man; she worshipped him and often followed him on his tours from continent to continent, reflecting in his glory and taking lessons whenever he had some free time. As she gushed on, I had a flash of recognition. Helga's odd, counterproductive arm movements *had* seemed vaguely familiar to me, as if I'd seen someone play like that before. Now I remembered; her famous teacher used exactly the same technique. But with one great difference: when he did it, it worked beautifully.

Some key discoveries have to be made for ourselves and cannot be passed along from teacher to student. Many techniques are neither good nor bad; their effectiveness depends entirely on who is using them, with what level of understanding, and whether the techniques happen to suit that person's body. It seemed to me that Helga's deferential "handmaiden" role with the great maestro had done nothing but arrest her own artistic growth, technical fluency, and ability to even *hear* her own playing.

MING

The story of "Ming" illustrates how good students can get stuck musically, and how they might become unstuck. Ming, a graduate piano student, was playing his Bach suite for the class. He had absorbed years of strict conservatory training in Asia: respect the teacher, never question, the music must be thus-and-so, get it exactly right, anything wrong will be ridiculed. Any suggestion by the teacher, even a casual remark, becomes a commandment of

How i do NOT WANT TO TEACH

sorts, an instant rule to be memorized and followed; the student must absorb the teacher's thought faithfully.

Even though interpretation of Western music is meant to be an opportunity for personal creativity, Ming was fixated on doing it correctly, according to the teacher's idea of correctness. As he played for the class, his listeners didn't feel much response . His playing, rather tight and hasty, did have some temperament, but only of a generic kind. We made suggestions to change this or that interpretive nuance, but every time he started the piece we sensed the same decisive mind-set, even before the first note; his playing was virtually the same each time.

What to do? I remembered a psychological technique I'd seen in a workshop. "Imagine that this is the International Bach Contest," I offered. "Everyone in the contest must play this very piece. The rendition we just heard was that of Contestant No. 14. We don't have any idea what the judges thought of it. Now we will hear someone from another part of the world play the piece—Contestant No. 38. This guy has quite different ideas—and maybe he's not so good!" Ming looked embarrassed and started again; not much different than before. I tried once more: "Contestant No. 22 is way off base—he takes the piece at *much* too slow a tempo." He risked this, playing the Bach "too" slowly.

We were all riveted. The counterpoint was absorbing, and his sound sprang to warm, human life. I tried to hide my grin of pleasure, because pleasing me was not the point. "Contestant No. 6 has the strange idea that this is a humorous piece," I threw out. He played with even more zest and communicative energy as he demonstrated this "silly" idea. Soon he didn't need our suggestions but continued to invent interesting versions which Ming would *never* do.

All the "wrong" interpretations had twice the musical vitality of Ming's customary dutiful-student approach. Which is best? At the moment, the question seemed unimportant. But who is Ming? That is more interesting. As long as he calls himself that name and takes the usual serious responsibility for his work, he seems the most predictable and uncreative of players. But as soon as he pretends to be someone else—a Hungarian or Brazilian or someone with questionable taste—he has freedom, imagination, and magnetism.

It wasn't going to be easy for Ming to know how to handle all these possibilities in the future as he prepared to perform and be evaluated. He'd have to redefine what it means to be a good student. He may feel tempted to revert to the safe old path—settling on one interpretation, anointing it as correct, and polishing it relentlessly while scorning all others. Or he may relax his hold, trust his momentary instincts, and dwell outside the "Ming" persona for a while. Either way, he had demonstrated to himself and his class-mates that he can indeed be a creative artist, capable of a multitude of fertile musical responses.

MELISSA

It is startling to see how easily a specific skill can be lost (or mis-placed) the moment a person is cast in the student role. I am think-ing in particular of the ability to count music correctly, to grasp and absorb rhythmic structure. Sixteen-year-old "Melissa" informs me dejectedly that she has always had a poor sense of rhythm. Every music teacher has told her so, and the assessment certainly seems borne out by the faulty counting she exhibits in my studio. Melissa's problem is by no means unique; many teenage students seem to share it. And difficulties with rhythm can be especially discourag-ing from the teacher's point of view, since a sense of rhythm is so fundamental, such an internal connection, so difficult for one per-son to correct in another.

Yet when I come across Melissa away from the music school, she appears to have no problem at all. Hanging out with a group of her friends and singing their favorite popular tunes together, songs which they have learned from the radio or recordings, she executes the most sophisticated, complex rhythms in perfect unison with the others. Rests, syncopations, quirky variations from one verse to the next, all are rendered flawlessly by every teenager. Of course their motivation for mastering music in this context is entirely different from that of the music lesson; this is the teens' own culture, it has nothing to do with a teacher, the music plays a role in the all-important social acceptance they hunger for, and in most cases—since they have never seen any written notation for the songs—they've learned them totally (and quite quickly) by ear.

Once again, vital musical abilities have gone into hiding in the studio. As with Helga and Ming, some sort of studentlike passivity seems to be the cause.

Perfectionism

Books on music pedagogy abound with reminders to maintain perfection at all points during the learning process. Many a piano teacher's studio wall is festooned with prim sayings extolling perfectionism, like the one I saw on a framed sampler recently: "Practice doesn't make perfect; perfect practice makes perfect." Whew! And yet if we widen our scope to include thinking from outside the studio, the value of perfectionism is called seriously into question. In *Gestalt Therapy Verbatim*, Perls states that if you are "cursed with perfectionism, you are absolutely sunk," and terms it the "beloved game of the neurotic, the self-torture game."[2]

Certainly this clash of views about perfectionism can be quite confusing, since there appears to be some truth on both sides of the issue. Depending on the context, perfectionism can apparently be a good trait or a destructive trait. For many young, high-achieving music students, the confusion can be intensified by family expectations and pressures. Once, after I had given a lecture to music educators entitled "Tension Problems of the Gifted Student," an audience member came up to me and said that I hadn't gone nearly far enough in describing the psychological stakes of musical perfectionism.

When she was a child, she said, if she didn't play Mozart on the piano flawlessly, she sensed that her mother simply didn't love her.

Parental expectations, so crucial to a child's psyche, can create perplexity for virtually any music student. The parents of toddlers greet their children's bumbling attempts at learning to walk with cheerful acceptance, support, smiles, and hugs. But take that same child and same parent, roll the imaginary tape forward several years, and picture the child practicing for a piano lesson in the den while the parent is busy in the kitchen. Child hits an obvious wrong note: an F-sharp that should have been an F. Parent calls out, "I heard that—be more careful! Your lesson is tomorrow, and we're paying good money for those lessons!" The parental view of imperfections seems to have reversed itself, yet the child no more meant to play a wrong note than he had meant to lose his balance as a toddler.

Perfectionistic expectations lead to detachment from one's body and a tendency to apologize preemptively for one's efforts, knowing from experience that there's sure to be something wrong with them. I make this statement because of a recurring exchange I've had with several students. The conversation is illogical—like a dialogue from *Alice in Wonderland*—which is why I have committed it to memory:

> TEACHER (after student plays awkward passage): How did that feel to you?
>
> STUDENT (glumly): I know that's not how it's supposed to sound.

Well, I wasn't talking about sound at all, or how it was "supposed to sound"! I was just asking how it felt physically. (And how did the phrase "supposed to" get into this discussion anyway?) Perfectionism can really get in the way of communication and perception, to say nothing of enjoyment and ultimate mastery.

Sight-reading and its dangers

Some people are born with a specific knack: to play music at sight with ease and with impressive results. Many good students, quick-witted and visually oriented, fall into this category. Not only can good sight-reading be a useful, marketable skill, it is further glorified by the chorus of praise (and envy) from those who find sight-reading a struggle. But good sight-readers often find themselves beset with troubles caused directly by their inappropriate use of this seemingly positive talent. They can develop physical tension—even injuries—and feel shaky in performance.

Why are they at risk? Because everything about sight-reading is technically unwholesome, according to the principles outlined in this book. If healthy playing is characterized by full awareness, relinquishing of control, and thorough physical commitment, sight-reading encourages the exact opposite. In fact, the very skill that makes sight-reading work is the narrowing of awareness, selectivity about what to be conscious of and what to ignore. Skillful sight-reading depends on more self-supervising, more self-consciousness, not less. And one can never play with physical thoroughness while sight-reading, because it is based on shrewd approximating—or, to put it more bluntly, faking. This is why, if you're planning to learn a particular piece of music, you shouldn't sight-read it very much or introduce sight-reading into your practicing. It simply confuses the body.

Deciding in an instant what to leave out (no one will notice), what to cleverly guess at, how to generalize and keep going, how to play by ear and camouflage the inevitable mistakes—these are the hallmarks of crafty sight-reading. Sight-readers have no choice but to be fixated on results—just finding the notes; never mind how it feels to get those results. They take every shortcut possible. Playing one measure while scanning the next one is a great technique for sight-reading, but disastrous for the holistic ideal of "experiencing the moment" because the sight-reader is experiencing *two* moments: the present and the future.

Sight-readers pretend to know, by playing in a pseudo-polished way, notes which their muscles don't in fact know at all, since there has been no chance to program the requisite motions with the patience that is so essential. In this respect, sight-reading is a lie. Physically, it is terribly ineffi-

> *The body simply doesn't like to lie or be lied to.*

cient as well; the same muscles and nerves which should be used for well-integrated *actions* are now used instead for *reactions*—hunting quickly and shallowly for the notes as quickly as the eye spots them, and playing tentatively just in case the eye happened to be mistaken. As a result, energy that should flow from the body-center out through the extremities now backs up, from clever fingers inward. This lack of good energy flow leads to muscle tension, incomplete playing, and a colorless tone quality.

Sight-reading distorts our perceptions about the music at hand. Quite frequently a passage that looks hard and is difficult to read turns out to be surprisingly easy to play; the two functions are not related. But if sight-reading is used as the initial point of departure, an inexperienced player can easily form the false notion that a particular passage is something to be feared. Such notions sink in and are difficult to change later.

In all these ways, the mind-body system is put so out of whack by sight-reading—especially when the material is complex—that it's practically impossible to prevent the buildup of harmful tension, even if one tries to think good thoughts about healthy posture, breathing, and relaxation while playing. The body simply doesn't like to lie or be lied to. This source of pervasive tension helps explain the distressingly high percentage of gifted, professional orchestral players who suffer from debilitating pain or injury caused by playing. Many say nothing about the problem for fear of losing their jobs. Many of these same players are prodigious sight-readers of the most demanding scores, and proud of that ability; in fact this is their stock in trade. There is certainly a direct link, although it has been very little discussed, between high-level sight-reading and performance injuries.

The ability to sight-read well can be enjoyable, and a major musical asset, and it makes sense to develop this skill. But to safeguard our health, we must do it for only brief periods of time and—most important—treat it as a separate musical activity entirely, not to be mingled with the technical learning of a piece.

The sight-reading dilemma dramatizes how crucial it is for the good student to cultivate inner honesty above all else. Or to look at it another way, solving this dilemma helps us to find out what inner honesty really means. When the good student chooses the honest path, free of perfectionism and faking, music study becomes something refreshingly new: a calm oasis of self-acceptance for those who are so used to driving themselves and trying to please others.

7 Out of Control, The Drama of Performing

Thoughtful, absorbed practicing can indeed create an oasis of serenity. But what happens when it's time to perform? Clearly, it is one thing to make music in private and quite another to do so onstage. And when I say "onstage" I mean it metaphorically; performing for two people in a living room can feel every bit as public as performing for two thousand in a hall.

We tend to undergo dramatic changes whenever our behaviors are framed as public performances. Telling a good joke in private, or voicing a passionate opinion to a friend—these are natural, colorful self-expressions. But if someone told us that television cameras would start rolling while we told the joke or expressed the opinion, we'd be "acting" and would probably feel stiff and artificial. Sometimes we even forget how to smile when we have to "perform" a smile; when a professional photographer asks us to smile naturally we inexplicably can't figure out which muscles we normally use, so we end up grimacing weirdly into the camera.

Physical skills, as well as personal expressions, feel different when there is an audience; as millions watch, the figure skater misses the triple jump she had landed perfectly in practice just moments before. Or the golfer misses the two-foot putt that would have won him the championship and million-dollar endorsement deals. This unpredictable immediacy of the present moment provides the very drama that makes sporting competitions so riveting to witness.

By and large, as individuals we're not used to being in the limelight. In many ways we are a society of consumers, leaving performance to high-level specialists—those accomplished professionals who clearly "deserve" to be on the stage. Furthermore, in musical contexts we've perpetuated a vocabulary that draws a line between the talented and the untalented, those who have a singing voice or don't, those who can or can't dance. Within this framework, many people would undoubtedly feel a bit presumptuous labeling themselves "musicians" and might very likely find the prospect of performing for an audience somewhat intimidating, or even ridiculous.

Yet part of us craves the stage, or so I believe. Many an adult music student announces at the start of lessons that he has no interest at all in trying to perform, only in playing some pieces "for my own enjoyment." But once his skills expand, his comfort and security grow, and his personal musical voice awakens, he becomes more open to being convinced (or perhaps prodded) to give a performance. And once he does perform a well-learned piece for others and in that moment senses new spontaneity and communication in the familiar notes, he experiences a wonderful and rare feeling: elation. Later he thanks the teacher for not paying too much attention to his earlier protestations.

In our culture of specialization, performance tends to be thought of as a big deal, an event that invites public scrutiny and critical judgment. This is not a viewpoint shared by all cultures, however. Apparently in certain tribal societies the spoken language contains no word that corresponds to musician. The reason is simple: they have no concept of a set-apart class of specialists who might be known as musicians as opposed to all the nonmusicians—virtually everyone in these tribal cultures, both young and old, is used to singing, dancing, and beating on drums

> *In certain tribal societies the spoken language contains no word that corresponds to* musician.

with communal spirit and without apology or fear. Apparently musical activity is accepted as normal and basic; music is considered an enjoyable component of life, of celebration, and of oneness with the tribe. But in industrialized society, the idea of performance is daunting to many people. Yet like all challenges, of course, it presents an opportunity.

Why bother with performing at all? For one thing, it's the crucial culminating step of the learning process, the capstone experience that pulls it all together. When you perform something well onstage, it is really part of you, in a way that no practice-room moment can duplicate. Even more importantly, performing means communicating with others, so music comes into its own as a magical language when it takes to the stage. It's the sharing of music that gives it its fullest meaning.

The ego in crisis

It's easy to sense that dramatic changes are underway when we go onstage. We feel the familiar physical symptoms driven by heightened adrenaline which we call nervousness: dry mouth, racing heartbeat, cold hands, perspiration, accelerated thoughts, overactive digestive processes. These are primal mammalian brain reactions that kick in whenever survival itself is at stake, and they are beautifully designed for the purpose. Hands get cold, for example, because if blood stays more around the vital organs and less in the extremities, we will survive longer if one of our limbs is caught in a trap or bitten off by a predator. As if we were cornered chipmunks, our racing thoughts and sped-up energy get us ready for either of the classic survival options: fight or flight.

But no one would claim that our physical survival is actually at stake if all we're about to do is get up in front of thirty-five friendly individuals and play *Sicilienne* on the flute, a Beethoven sonata on the piano, or sing "Ol' Man River." Yet many find themselves filled with visceral panic as they are about to go on (in fact, when I was competing once in a major international piano competition we were rather alarmingly informed that medical personnel would be on call backstage, should a contestant suffer a breakdown). So something else must be operating here—some significant fear that seems as momentous to the brain as survival itself. There must be a good reason why, according to many studies, fear of public speaking is one of the greatest fears human beings have. I think the underlying fear can be easily identified: losing control in front of others, and facing the possibility of embarrassment and humiliation.

Something new is going to happen and we don't know what. It might be very good, or it might be very bad. Either way, it will be a surprise—we seem to have utterly relinquished control over events. We tend to feel physically peculiar too; when I chat with a music student and ask if she ever feels, when stepping onstage, as if she had been transformed into an outer-space android with a totally different nervous system in place of the usual one, she always knows what I'm talking about. We do tend to feel that way, disconnected and odd, at least in the first moments of a performance—until we find a groove, hit our stride, or as the French say, "ease into the bath."

When I think of the performing experience and how it affects us, I picture a delicate transparent shell around the performer, like a clear, pliable bubble or membrane. This is the shell of ego, the protective shell of a person feeling in control, navigating through various everyday situations in life. Most of the time we depend on the existence of that shell (imaginary as it may be) as our refuge whenever we might need it, our invisible armor, our personal zone of privacy. But that shell cannot stay intact onstage, where we voluntarily get up in front of others and make ourselves the focus of attention, and this is what we sense in advance, instinctively, about the nakedness of performing. Will our fears cause the shell to harden, become brittle, and shatter? Will we fumble unnervingly and feel humiliated? Or will the shell happily melt away, permitting our musical impulses to soar trustingly out into the room with newfound energy, joining meaningfully with the receptive spirit of the audience? In any event, something new and exposing will happen as soon as we sense that this is the official performance, that "This is it."

There's a remarkable feeling of aliveness and connection which we are all capable of but (unfortunately) rarely feel; it's often referred to as "living in the moment." One thing is sure: to get up onstage and perform is to plunge oneself instantly into living in the moment.

Nerves

The feeling of nervousness that performers have is not a feeling that many people are used to. Thus, we may fear and dislike the word *nervous* and all that it implies. Of course it only adds to our general agitation if what we're nervous about is nervousness itself!

Finding a way to frame the same physical sensations with different, more encouraging words can ease our fears greatly. Why not think of our hyper-energy, cold hands, and rapid thoughts as symptoms of excitement and anticipation? Most experienced performers will say that they still get nervous before every show, but they often add that they welcome the feeling, finding it essential to the heightened focus and alertness that are hallmarks of vital performing. Undoubtedly they have, consciously or subconsciously, found a positive conceptual framework for the aroused physical state we think of as nervousness.

Fight-or-flight symptoms are an uncommon experience for modern people, since for most of us primal survival is not a danger-ridden daily issue. Our ancestors may have risked their lives hunting mastodons (nervously) in order to eat, but we drive to the supermarket. Yet our brain's wiring hasn't changed much, and human survival responses are still triggered by the idea that we are under imminent threat. Since this is a rare event, we may easily overreact when those feelings occur.

Another, perhaps less obvious, reason we find the nervous state distressing is that we're not accustomed to being held accountable in the dramatized way that is part of every public performance. Public performance is a potent truth serum, stripping away all self-delusions and instantly revealing—in front of an audience—the solidity of our knowledge, our precise degree of mastery. All bets are off when we step onstage, and things usually don't happen exactly as rehearsed or predicted. What thoroughly integrated learning it takes, both in body and mind, to welcome such accountability with confidence!

> *Public performance is a potent truth serum.*

By contrast, if you are taking a spelling test, you can pace yourself—stop and think for a moment before committing to a particular answer. You can take time to retrieve your knowledge. If we could do this with music, there would be no issue of nerves. But while spelling is mental, musical performance is physical *and* mental, and it gives you no extra time to think. It would obviously ruin the possible magic of a performance if we were to stop abruptly in the middle of a phrase, stand up, and say to the audience, "Sorry, folks, I really messed up that last passage (which surprises me since just half an hour ago I played it perfectly during the warm-up)—so let me take another shot at it, OK? Thanks!" No; since the flow of sound mustn't stop, we find ourselves profoundly accountable both to the music and to the audience.

One little-discussed and surprisingly beneficial aspect of performance nerves has to do precisely with this accountability. The unconscious mind, uncannily aware, knows when there are loose ends—such as incomplete memorization or a technical passage that's been learned too shallowly to be secure in performance. Something must be done to tie up the loose end, but the conscious mind has refused to pay any attention to the matter during practice—perhaps it's not even aware that there's a potential problem. So the unconscious tugs at our sleeve, using the symptoms of nervousness, saying, "Please, for your own sake, take another look! Right now, before you step onstage! Don't assume you really know this!" In this instance, nerves are functioning as an effective stratagem for self-protection. If we try to cajole ourselves out of nervousness using generalized feel-good psychological techniques, we miss its pragmatic, helpful message and (later) pay the consequences.

Admittedly, getting the message only moments before we walk onstage doesn't give us much time to respond—although many a performance has indeed been saved backstage, ten minutes before curtain time, by someone listening carefully to nerves and studying a specific spot that was shaky. The more useful response in the long term is to realize that honest, thorough practicing greatly reduces the need for this type of nervousness.

Just as there is plenty to be learned from mistakes, once we put our egos aside, there is also much to be learned from nerves. I remember clearly the occasion on which I was the most nervous in my life: my first concert as a concerto soloist with orchestra. In retrospect, I'm glad that I got so nervous; the nerves

> *Once we put our egos aside, there is much to be learned from nerves.*

helped me learn more in one night than I ever could have learned from a teacher or from practicing.

I was an eighteen-year-old college student and had just won, much to my amazement, my first concerto competition. The award was a performance as soloist with a community orchestra before an audience of about two thousand people. Although I was a novice at formal concerts and had never performed a concerto before, the two pieces I played were comfortable to me, and all had gone surprisingly well up to this point—the lessons, the audition, the rehearsals with conductor and orchestra. But there's nothing quite like an actual performance, as I was about to find out.

Concert night arrived. I put on the tuxedo and strode out onstage, feeling like a piece of petrified wood. The work was Mendelssohn's *Capriccio brillant* in B minor, op. 22, which starts (luckily) with a safely undemanding slow section, lyrical and expressive. Although my fingers felt stiff and alien, I was riveted on the task at hand and the music sounded perfectly OK. But then came the fast "brilliant" part. That started to go well too, although the fast tempo fueled my adrenaline more than I needed it to, which in turn made the tempo even faster. But despite the precipitous speed, I began to enjoy the occasion more, breathe more calmly, and allow my ego to take an interest. Soon my thoughts were drifting pleasantly away from Mendelssohn's familiar notes and toward my own situation, and I was reflecting on how nicely things were going and fantasizing about the rousing ovation I hoped to hear at the end. I was definitely no longer "in the moment."

> *The daydream vanished, I plunged back into reality, and the nerves hit again.*

It was during a rapid but quite simple transition figure of repeated sixteenth-notes (after several decades, I still know the exact spot in the score) that the daydream vanished, I plunged back into reality, and the nerves hit again, all at once. This time, though, the nerves were on a mission: they wanted solid data, and they wanted it now. I heard a strange voice in my head—a part of my mind I'd never heard from before. This nasal, crisp, robotic inner voice wasted no time on small talk. It fired questions at me in an insistent, machine-gun style: "How many times is this figure repeated, is it going down or up, what key are you in, what key are you going to, what exactly happens next?" In highly condensed brain-time these questions were posed all in the same instant, but they were crystal clear nonetheless.

It was equally clear that I was doomed to flunk the quiz, didn't know a single answer. But hadn't I played the piece over and over in the past without a hitch? Yes. Didn't that prove I knew the piece? Well, I *thought* I did.

Let's freeze the movie frame for a second, and take a look at what was really happening. The passage in question is actually so uncomplicated, and fits under the hands so naturally, that I'd never given it a lot of thought. I'd learned it in ten minutes and usually just let muscular habit and my good musical ear guide me down the familiar pathway. But as soon as I heard the list of robot-questions onstage, I felt pure panic, because I instantly grasped the way in which I was unprepared. The questions themselves were 100 percent fair. This wasn't neurotic self-tormenting on my part; this was a straightforward request for factual information about the piece I was presenting, which, as a well-prepared performer, I should have known. It was my job to know the piece cold, to be able to recite all its musical data without touching a piano.

Had I learned it in that way, I wouldn't ever find myself onstage grasping at tactile, visual, or auditory kinds of memory—all of which function automatically and strongly but are also primal functions that can't stand up to questioning: the tactile, visual, and auditory memories can evaporate at any time. They come easily; therefore they can go away easily. But exercising one's left brain to name every note and analyze all the patterns, without looking at a score or touching an instrument, is productive work. It's a bracing mental workout that solidifies the memory by actively retrieving information from the recesses of one's own mind. This process

145

is radically different from the simple, passive act of *recalling* how familiar music goes.

Similarly, a successful academic student knows that active studying is infinitely more effective than passive reading. For example, asking a friend to test you on the twenty-five vocabulary words (and to jump around the list, so the quiz won't be too easy) will cause you to retrieve the definitions from your own head, thus giving you the certainty of knowledge that leads to solid confidence under pressure. But just reading over the words and thinking, "Yes, these certainly do look familiar" calls for no retrieval of information at all; this is passive studying and poor preparation.

Since we know with certainty that we *will* question ourselves onstage, we simply aren't prepared until we've created the sort of solid musical memory that will stand up well under serious pressure.

All this was clear to me in an instant. It was also clear that I would have needed no more than five minutes offstage to study that passage sufficiently to answer the quiz with ease. But I hadn't done that—hadn't seen the need—and now I was being held accountable. That attack of nerves was in fact highly beneficial, teaching me a practical lesson which gave me far greater onstage security in the years that followed. I wouldn't have paid any attention to the lesson if I hadn't been trying to "survive" in front of two thousand people.

And now to resume the movie: somehow I managed to salvage the moment by jumping ahead a couple of beats to the next theme—or what I fervently hoped was the next theme. Luckily this episode occurred right before a place in the music where the orchestra is silent for half a page, which enabled the conductor to figure out where I was so we could get back together quickly. I'd like to think that what the audience noticed was at most a minor glitch, but to me it was a turning point in understanding the job of preparing for performance.

Performance nerves illustrate what music study has to offer: an adventurous journey of knowing. We discover that knowing is dynamic, not fixed from day to day. Frequently our grasp of the piece at hand turns out to be shallower than we had thought, not quite integrated enough. This is humbling and at the same time inspiring. This sense of knowing as an adventure could easily apply to philosophical or spiritual quests, but the great boon of stage experience is that it brings immediate reality to a concept that might otherwise seem quite vague. The act of performing almost forces us to become our best selves: performers must be realists, rise to the occasion, and shed limitations such as self-delusions, narcissism, and unproductive thoughts. Our minds must unite intuition and rationality in a purposeful, high-level way. We must make sense of the abstract. We must become fluid, open-system thinkers, always receptive to new connections. If learning to play a particular piece of music is a journey, then that journey of knowledge isn't quite complete without the culminating stage of public performance—even if it's for an audience of one.

Expansiveness

Up to now, this chapter has focused inward, on the challenges and opportunities for the performer. But equally significant is the outward focus, the aspect of sharing and connecting with others through music's uncanny powers of enchantment.

As it happens, the expansive side of performing also became real to me during that same performance years ago. My second piece of the evening was the Rimsky-Korsakov Piano Concerto, op. 30, and I had calmed down appreciably by that time (no more daydreams, fortunately). The solo cadenza toward the end of this concerto is always a favorite of mine because of the relaxed, improvisatory warmth of the writing. Something intriguing happened when I got to that spot in performance.

Until that moment, I hadn't thought very philosophically about what expression in performance really meant: I thought my role was to "offer my interpretation" of the music to the audience, whom I hoped would find it acceptable and demonstrate their approval of me with respectful silence during the music and

> It was a sense of effortless collective power—not my own power at all.

applause (thunderous, please) afterward. However, I now sensed something different; the collective awareness, the attentive mind of the audience, was a tangible, mutual bond of energy linking me, the soloist, with two thousand listeners. Actors and other performers know this feeling, but it was new to me and I'd never thought of it before. It was a sense of effortless collective power—not my own power at all.

I seemed to be plugged into a meaningful circuit, a circuit made up of many elements: the composer's thought, my response to it, the piano, my hands, and the audience's individual and collective feelings. All the components energized each other and formed a pattern. This was a reversal in perception; my fears before going onstage had stemmed more from the sense of separateness—the austere formality of the stage, my isolated role as soloist under the lights, and the physical and psychological distance all this created between me and "them." Even family and friends were temporarily part of the anonymous "them."

But once I accepted the alone-ness of the stage, stopped fearing it, and stopped trying to protect my ego from its imagined dangers, it began to feel surprisingly comfortable and enriching. I felt one with the piano, relaxed and trusting. I realized that my connection with the audience had become intimate, nourishing, and boundless. And as for interpretation, I was receiving as much as I was giving; there no longer seemed to be a fixed, intact item known as "my interpretation." Clearly, the expressive intentions I had

worked out in solitary practice were merely preparations, pale out-
lines of what I now felt (knew) were the fuller meanings the communal circuit was creating.

Here's another example of the same sort of experience, outside
the realm of music. Let's say you've been asked to tell a dramatic
story to a kindergarten class. You practice it at home, working out
your timing, inflections, and gestures. But when you find yourself in
front of the children, telling it for real, something unexpected may
happen. If you've managed to capture their rapt attention, if you see
the engaged gleam in their eyes, you may be transformed. Suddenly
you are freer, more commanding, more creative in your narrating
style—forget all the planned gestures!—and you also find yourself
grasping for the first time the story's true power and meaning. The
circuit is complete, they're bringing this flow out of you, and you
can't go wrong (unless of course you break the circuit by thinking
too much about your own wonderful performance).

Thus part of the enrichment we get from performing is a discovery—the sense that artistic understanding is not only a solo
journey for the performer but a communal wisdom that transcends
his or her personal boundaries.

The stage is full of surprises and brings primal immediacy to
every moment. In *The Hidden Face of Music*, Herbert Whone says
about performance:

> In the animal world we see a potent stillness which
> appears to delay the attack until the last moment; for the
> string player it is the stillness of the bow . . . for the pianist
> it is the hand raised in still suspense above the keyboard,
> and for the singer or wind player it is the control of deli-
> cately withheld breath. It is a sense of delay before an
> entry which gives a heightened awareness—an awareness
> that belongs to the forest, to the prickling of ears, to

stealth and the cracking of twigs. To be immediate, means to be animal . . . the musician as well as the athlete would do well to study this part of his being. The art of immediacy is the art of no mediation—of the elimination of all that stands in the way of pure action. It is a life work.[1]

The ego-drama of performance can be visualized in terms of where energy is directed. Onstage nerves are often driven by thoughts of "What do you all think of me?" Performing for a panel of judges in a music contest can also make a musician of any age fixate on "What do you think of me?" Such thoughts of powerlessness can cause a physical sense of constriction, as if one's shoulders were being squeezed. It's as if all the energy in the room, all the scrutiny, were pointing in at the performer, as the arrows in the diagram suggest.

The constriction of "What do you think of me?"

But to embrace performing and its possibilities means to reverse the direction of those arrows. Instead of the anxious egoism of "What do you all think of me?" we can convert to the generosity of "Let me share this with you" and the receptivity of "What does this mean to all of us, right in this moment?" Then the circuit of energy in the room becomes complete.

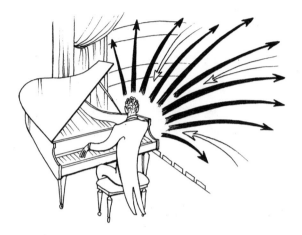

Sending energy out, completing the performer-audience circuit

To sense performance energy as a bond with others is among the greatest rewards a person can have. For that to happen, the pathway to fulfillment must be open, free of roadblocks. This raises questions about music lessons: what can teachers do to encourage self-trust in students, both onstage and off? The next chapter considers lessons from the teacher's point of view.

8 | *Lessons and Un-Lessons*

It's invigorating to feel freedom and self-trust. Certainly music lessons can and should provide just such an experience to the student. But to maintain the vitality and effectiveness of lessons, we would do well to rethink their workings from time to time.

Curiously, students don't always like it when we teachers try to revamp our educational philosophy. The perfectionistic, prescriptive music-teacher persona is so entrenched in the general cultural perception that students may continue to cast us in the role of omniscient dictator no matter what we say or do. Students usually come around to a new approach eventually, but sometimes this can take a little while.

This resistance to change can certainly be a puzzlement to the teacher. Who wouldn't want to find new ways to become an effective, autonomous problem-solver in music? Who wouldn't choose honest practicing, if it meant feeling more comfortable, freely artistic, and self-confident in performance? One answer is that mental passivity is a lot less work than self-reliance is, and the easy path is always tempting—even if we're repeatedly disappointed in where it takes us. To accept responsibility, to achieve and maintain total self-honesty, requires mental energy, focus, and—above all—a kind of courage.

Teachers thus have a meaningful opportunity: to inspire that courage in students by creating an atmosphere in which courage can thrive. It's helpful to set a tone in lessons that is cheerful, lively, adventurous, and collaborative. Teachers can show through their actions that one can pursue a high standard of excellence with integrity and still keep a sense of humor. If students see a teacher brainstorming solutions with gusto, thereby modeling optimism and energy, the students will more likely want to join in that process. Such vitality of mind and spirit is contagious and exudes— more than words or logic ever can—the attractive promise of break- throughs to come.

But in addition to setting the overall tone, teachers can avail themselves of some good strategies. Most of the strategies I'm about to suggest share a key characteristic: they contain some sort of par-

> *Vitality of mind and spirit is contagious.*

adox, or they turn convention on its head in some way. That's why I think of them as "Un-lessons." Un-lessons are seemingly off-the-wall approaches that are likely to surprise (or even annoy) the perfectionistic "good student," who may consider paradoxical ideas pointless at first, or even counterproductive. This is exactly why they are so refreshing and effective.

In analyzing the workings of the creative process, several writ- ers have referred to an old French phrase, *Reculer pour mieux sauter*. Literally this means "to back up in order to jump farther."[1] Sometimes the most productive next step does seem to be a step in precisely the wrong direction. But with any luck, it will arouse per- fectionists' curiosity, causing them to be more and more intrigued.

Turn the project upside down

In music practice, it's always effective to isolate a problem. But sometimes the problem itself needs to be reframed, redefined, reduced skillfully to a subproblem, in order for progress to take place. Douglas Hofstadter, physicist and author of *Gödel, Escher, Bach*, points out that there is definitely an art to "problem-reduc- tion," or what my old piano teacher invariably referred to as Divide and Conquer. The art is in defining the subgoals thoughtfully, and we may be surprised at times by the directions they take us.

Hofstadter gives this example: a dog is playing in a backyard, separated by a wire fence from the neighbor's yard. Someone throws a juicy, delicious bone onto the neighbor's grass, right across from where the dog is. The dog can see the bone through the fence, and it's just a few feet away. There also happens to be an open gate in the fence, but it's way off to the dog's right, about fifty feet away from the bone.

> What do you do? Some dogs will just run up to the fence, stand next to it, and bark; others will dash . . . to the open gate and double back to the lovely bone. Both dogs can be said to be exercising the problem reduction technique; however, they represent the problem in their minds in different ways, and this makes all the difference. The barking dog sees the subproblems as (1) running to the fence, (2) getting through it, and (3) running to the bone—but that second subproblem is a "toughie"; whence the barking. The other dog sees the subproblems as (1) getting to the gate; (2) going through the gate; (3) running to the bone. Notice how everything depends on the way you represent the "problem space"—that is, on what you perceive as *reducing* the problem (forward motion toward the overall goal) and what you perceive as *magnifying* the problem (backward motion away from the goal).[2]

In music we often have to move decisively away from the "luscious" bone—the goal—in order to eventually reach it. For example, if the goal is to control an ethereal *pianissimo* passage, it won't help much (although it *will* create a lot of shoulder tension) to strive each day to play it ever more *pianissimo*; we'll start cramping up, pulling back, and losing the energy flow. What does work is to practice it loudly, freely, and rambunctiously, just the opposite of what the score calls for. The reason is simple: in order to control the quietest sounds—one of the trickiest aspects of any technique—we must have attained a thoroughly comfortable feeling with the notes. I always think of this as "making friends" with the notes, and to achieve that comfort we usually have to play with a big, relaxed commitment—at first. This makes the muscles happy, removes tension and frustration, and encourages the body to trust the passage enough to take the weight out of it later. The wonderful boon is that in this "new" sort of *pianissimo* there is no harmful tension, and when there's no tension you can do almost anything.

Similarly, if the music is slow, practice it fast, with a certain recklessness. If it calls for great evenness, make it enthusiastically uneven and vary the patterns. When there is serenity of body and mind, these counter-strategies work with amazing efficiency. But can we really give ourselves permission to go in such a "wrong" direction? It's not always so easy. Using Hofstadter's analogy, the skilled problem solver *should* turn away from the bone and run over to the gate:

> But dogs in front of fences sometimes have a hard time doing that, especially when that bone is sitting there so close, staring them in the face, and looking so good. And when the problem space is just a shade more abstract than physical space, people are often just as lacking in insight about what to do as the barking dogs.[3]

And if we do follow the zigzag path of the more enlightened dog, will others approve? That can get tricky. I've seen students who take this common-sense approach held up to public ridicule by prominent teachers, who admonish that under no circumstances should one ever stray from the composer's artistic intentions, even in practice.

Eloise Ristad's thought-provoking insights into teaching included lots of inventive, often paradoxical ways to redefine problems. In *A Soprano on Her Head* (which is itself as upside-down an image as one could ask for) she sets out to help a piano student who greatly desired more power in her playing:

> "Without trying for more power, sense your solar plexus as
> you play." She had been trying to get power from her arms
> and shoulders rather than from a source deep within her
> body. "Now sense the bones you sit on as they contact the
> piano bench." She settled deeper into her body. "Now
> sense the limitations of power as you play." As she
> searched for limitations, the limitations began to vanish,
> and she became engrossed in surprising sensations of
> increased power.[4]

I once asked Eloise what to do if I have to perform on an ugly-toned piano when I'm traveling. Her answer, typically unexpected, has proven quite helpful: "Don't fight it or make compensations while you play; just explore, be fascinated, and learn everything you can about the exact nature of that piano's ugliness." Body and mind ease as a result of such acceptance, focus becomes specific, self-conflict lessens, and the sounds starts to bloom.

In Betty Edwards's *Drawing on the Right Side of the Brain* we find an inspiring example of turning a task upside down (literally) in order to trick one's brain into succeeding at it. In this case an elegant, stylized line drawing by a famous artist is printed in the book—upside down. The reader is invited to settle in, take lots of time, remove all distractions, and just copy all the abstract lines and curves, not trying to recognize or render any specific objects that may be part of the upside-down image. Once that is done to one's satisfaction, the picture is turned right side up. I did the exercise and was stunned to see the result: an assured, sophisticated drawing which I could hardly believe my "untalented" drawing hand could possibly have produced. Edwards theorizes that the left brain—bossy, literal-minded, and ambitious—actively dislikes any tasks that seem pointless and silly. So the left brain disdainfully resigns from such projects, thus clearing the way for the more instinctive right brain to take over.[5]

Remove the goal

Another approach extends the same theme, but with a slightly different focus. In addition to breaking down a goal into effective and creative subgoals, we can sometimes remove the goal altogether and still reap exciting rewards.

I have an American friend who has lived and worked for many years in Asia, speaking and reading Mandarin Chinese every day with amazing ease and fluency. One day I asked her how she had managed that feat of learning. She cited several factors, including enthusiasm for the task, daily practice, and freedom from distractions. But the experience that seemed to have opened the door to her future linguistic success had nothing to do with Mandarin Chinese at all. She had undergone a brief training and orientation course many years before, run by the agency that was about to send her and other educators to remote parts of the globe. The teachers were all poised to begin language study for their various destinations. But before they were permitted to do so, each teacher was required to take an intensive class—for one full week—in a *different* language, one they knew nothing about and had no intention of ever learning. In my friend's case, this was an exotic-sounding African language full of loud clicks and other sounds to which she was unaccustomed.

Like the perfectionistic straight-A student she had always been, she immediately thought the requirement a pointless waste of time. But a breakthrough was about to happen. While she had always excelled academically in high school Spanish, she acknowledged that her ear for that language had been mediocre. Now, with nothing to remember and no quizzes, grades, or goals, she discovered something new about learning a new language: it's fun. It was fun to experiment with wild new sounds, without any embarrassment, and she soon came to believe that she could successfully mimic any vocal sound she heard. It had become a game, pure and simple. Her language "ear" had opened, and language study had become a delightful adventure. By the next week, when she turned to Chinese, she was ready to absorb in a brand new way.

What's the musical analog? Improvisation. Making up one's own music with no finished product, no goal except the enjoyment of exploration. Improvisation uses musical sounds as spontaneous human language. It can be done in structured ways or in free, totally unstructured ways (atonal improvisation is probably the easiest and most fun); it can be done alone or in a group. Improvisation is not composition; there is usually no intention to remember the music afterward. In improvisation we celebrate the fleeting moment, and relish the opportunity to be inventive, responsive, ridiculous, colorful, fresh, artistic, and—above all—genuine. Group improvisation provides an especially rich opportunity; few interpersonal bonds are as satisfying as the playful, mischievous pleasure shared by several people who have just improvised something that seems to them just right, something really "cool." That music emerged from their openness to each other and trust in each moment, so it had no single author, no committee chairman, and no single owner. The inevitable shared belly-laugh that follows such dynamic experiences is a sure sign of release and liberation. In his book *Free Play*, Stephen Nachmanovitch says of this flowing new freedom, "The noun of self becomes a verb."[6]

It's easy to see how improvising, which awakens the spontaneous musical self, can bring life and immediacy to one's playing of Bach, Stravinsky, or any other composer. Yet, not surprisingly, those of us who have been system-dependent good students are often stricken with panic when asked to improvise for the first time. That would mean giving up all control, and we have much to lose (or think we do). I like to use bongo drums, vocal sounds, any nonperfectionistic means I can find to help students get comfortable with this activity. Removing goals—even the goal of improvising well—feels very odd at first, but the paradox is well worth exploring for the benefits of alertness and joy in music making that it can yield.

Try the (seemingly) impossible

Good students have usually found clever ways to protect themselves, to avoid the unaccustomed embarrassment or anxiety of being stumped by a problem. All they have to do is profess distaste for the music or boredom with the project, and most likely the teacher will let them off the hook. In many cases, the underlying truth is that the students are actually afraid of failing, even though they are probably not aware of this and would never admit it.

On certain occasions, though, a teacher may decide to stand firm and insist that a particular project be done. If the existing teacher-student relationship has been an easygoing and democratic one, the student will be somewhat surprised by this autocratic behavior, but that's all right; surprise is an excellent way to get a student's attention. Why would a teacher take a risk like this? To nudge the student into the deep end of the pool, help him discover that he really can swim in water over his head. Sometimes people secretly want to be nudged into the deep, despite their balking; in fact this may be one of their most interesting reasons for seeking out music lessons in the first place.

One of my favorite examples of the "deep end" is the pianistic phenomenon of polyrhythms, wherein each hand plays a mathematically uneven number of notes simultaneously. One hand might spread out seven notes in exactly the same time-span that the other plays four, for instance. This seems like quite a tricky feat, baffling to those who have never managed it; in fact, until you've played polyrhythms they may seem close to impossible. Here is a polyrhythm, from a beautiful Chopin prelude (see measure 4), which has stumped many a smart, high-achieving piano student (Example 10).

Example 10. Chopin, Prelude in F-sharp major, op. 28, no. 13, beginning.

Five against six. Situations like this always remind me of an acquaintance, a chemistry professor, who is a fluent amateur pianist obsessed with trying to play Chopin's polyrhythms. He can never figure them out using his proficient problem-reducing left brain; thus he has convinced himself that success will never be possible for him. He's probably too caught up in the mathematics of polyrhythms to consider a radically different way of thinking. To me, this challenge exemplifies an exciting threshold—just the sort of mental liberation which music study can offer.

My professor friend and other good students will probably think something like this when faced with five against six:

1. I've never seen this before; I've got to calculate the ratio mathematically so I'll know how to line up the notes properly.

2. Five into six doesn't go; since there's no common denominator I'll have to multiply out to thirty and carefully insert each note on the appropriate one-thirtieth of the measure.

Some have proceeded with this daunting plan, even going so far as to make detailed charts. But this effort leads them inevitably to the next realization:

3. Step 2 is impossible!

Which it is. Not only is mastering a subdivision of thirty totally unwieldy, but in musical terms we wouldn't even want such a fixed, robotic, self-conscious rendering of the phrase. In fact, the reason romantic composers like Brahms and Chopin wrote lots of polyrhythms was to create a dreamy, poetic sort of independence between the hands (although they do have to start and end together!). It's all part of the romantics' love of the mystical, the irrational, and the emotional.

In fact, in Example 10, the six left-hand notes would usually be played quite calmly and evenly as a soothing cushion of sound over which the right hand can be freely expressive, quasi-improvisatory. The rhythmic relationship between the hands should be a liberated one, not a rigid one. Thus the right hand's five notes might not be played evenly at all, but might linger at the beginning and rush forward a bit at the end of the measure—or linger in the middle or at the end of the figure. It really doesn't matter. Ideally, a player would feel free to pace the phrase differently every time, letting the right-hand timing take shape in the intimate moment of performance. So what are we seeking here? Not exactitude, but a much freer sort of mastery.

This passage is a prime example of the "irrational" in music. By this I mean a passage which the body can learn readily but which the mind will never be equipped to figure out. I do believe that certain people seek out musical challenges because they are hungry for exactly this type of experience: they want to integrate the irrational, open up a new realm of understanding, and give their controlling minds a rest.

Learning such a passage is a simple matter, as it turns out. Naturally, the key to success is trust—just the opposite of all those obsessive mathematical calculations. All the pianist has to do is learn each hand's part well, then set up a steady large beat (the beat that will contain all five or six notes) that is not too slow: we need some rhythmic swing and momentum to do this. Relax, breathe, play a few right-hand phrases, then a few left-hand phrases, always conforming to the same large beat. Now and then, without thinking, throw the hands together and see if they come out at the same time. The body will negotiate this after just a few tries; it's really not a very hard coordination, as most people delightedly discover. But the good-student brain will never be able to explain how the coordination works, and this in itself is a pleasant—if rather odd—new feeling for many students.

Another seemingly impossible task has to do with atonal music. Many students are convinced it would be impossible to memorize, and swear they have no interest in performing it. Too ugly, too weird, too confusing, they will say. But here again, if the teacher senses that this is a good moment to insist, the stage may be set for a major learning breakthrough.

Skillful memorizing normally uses lots of traditional harmonic information as an essential mental guide. While we play, an internal narration takes place, such as: Here I am on a G minor chord, now my bass line is moving down by steps, I pass through C minor and this diminished chord and end up on the V-chord. Once the basic theory vocabulary is there, all these handy chord labels and relationships can be learned and stored in the mind. But how could anyone mentally summarize a passage, for example, from Arnold Schoenberg's *Klavierstücke*, op. 11 (Example 11)?

Example 11. Schoenberg, *Klavierstücke*, op. 11, no. 1, mm. 35–37.

These note combinations can't be labeled in conventional harmonic language. Luckily, though, musical memory is a flexible blend of several different memory modes: visual, tactile, auditory, spatial (overview), analytical (detail). This blend can be adjusted according to what's needed. In the case of atonal music, analytical memory won't help much since there isn't any familiar chord vocabulary to hang your hat on. Trying to commit to memory the name of every note, or the size of every interval between the notes, is a simplistic, tedious, and arbitrary task; and such a mountain of data would be hard to retain anyway. But a more general picture, a kind of bird's eye overview of the music's form, would be extremely helpful; to this purpose, one can create (mentally or on paper) a picture loosely representing the shapes and gestures in the music. Furthermore, although our ears may have trouble identifying the atonal relationships, our fingers probably have vital information. Muscle memory, as strong as it is, can't normally be trusted all by itself, since it's an unthinking sort of memory and can shut off at any time. But why not set out deliberately to make physical memory a bigger than usual ingredient in this new memory recipe? It's a lot of fun to practice aggressively, with the intention of making the intervals and shapes as physically concrete as they can possibly be.

Once we've done that, what do we have? An overall mental map of the textures, shapes, and forms; a concrete physical feel for the piece; and we may add a few key notes memorized in detail by rote (just to give us reminders in case we get stuck). Now we're ready to present the piece convincingly. This brings me to one of the unique and inviting properties of atonal music: if you happen to forget a note or two in performance and need to make something up just to keep going, most of your audience will never know as long as you carry it off with dramatic conviction. To the perfectionist, this may seem deliciously subversive, but it's just a practical fact. A wrong note in Schoenberg will never be as noticeable to the general audience as a wrong note in Mozart.

Atonal music invites the performer to be free in two specific ways: first, trusting more in "primitive" types of memory, and second, communicating the piece as an actor would—through gesture and drama. Ironically, it's the very strangeness of the music that makes it so liberating. When a performance of atonal music works well, there is real electricity between performer and audience; listeners find it a fresh experience because they can't predict what's going to happen next. The performer feels less anxious about the occasional mistake (which won't be that obvious) and freer to cut loose dramatically (the notes may not communicate all by themselves; the performer has to act them out with flair in order to involve the audience). Many times I've seen an exciting transformation from dutiful student to riveting performer, thanks to an "impossible" atonal music assignment and the new resources it brought out in a budding musician.

Brainstorm the possibilities

Musicians often voice the truism that there is no single, best interpretation of a given piece. There are many valid and beautiful ways to penetrate to the heart of the music at hand. But while we think this and say it, we don't always act on it in the teaching studio. It's all too convenient to dictate prefabricated solutions to students, shaping the students in our own image. After all, aren't we supposed to know more than they do, and isn't that sort of guidance exactly what they seem to expect?

Again the issue is essentially one of vitality. How can students awaken and grow musically if they are trying to perfect a second-hand rendition of someone else's interpretive instinct? I remember a national piano teachers' conference that was galvanized by provocative questions posed at the outset by the guest keynoter, bassoonist and educator John Steinmetz. Referring to the numerous teaching demonstrations which the attendees would be watching in the days to come, Steinmetz suggested: "As you observe the two people onstage, teacher and student, ask yourself: Does one seem to have more energy than the other? Who's having the most fun? Who's making discoveries?" The silence that followed was a pensive and uneasy one.

If we do want students to make discoveries, our intentions must be pure; we must mean it. If "discovery" turns out to be just disguised ways of guiding them, they become understandably apathetic, resenting the deceptiveness of such an approach.

Happily, there is much to discover about pieces of music, even the most familiar ones. When we say that many effective interpretations are possible, we usually mean that different people can respond differently, but with equal validity. But it's also true that one person can respond in various ways; this is what I call interpretive brainstorming.

As an example, let's take the first measures of Debussy's evocative flute solo *Syrinx*, as shown in Example 12. These simple, haunting notes certainly require some imagination; it is up to each performer to bring variety, meaning, and shape to the work. The first phrase repeats at A. If it's played just the same as the first time, the music will sound too planned, not very alive. But just how should the two phrases differ?

Example 12. Debussy, *Syrinx* for solo flute, beginning. Opening phrase repeats at A.

Countless good answers are possible here. A teacher might suggest, "Play the first one wistfully, then make the repeat more urgent," which is perfectly fine, but it's only one solution out of many. And with too much repetition any fixed interpretation will probably become stale. Better to withhold suggestions and appeal to creativity; ask the student to brainstorm three different approaches to the two phrases, each with a contrasting pair of personalities. See if the student can make you guess correctly what contrasts were intended—dreamy/insistent, lamenting/echoing, seductive/shy, for example. Be honest, though; if they all sound alike, say so. Once you've heard some colorful contrasts, don't express an immediate preference; ask if the student liked one version best, and honor that choice—students need to test their own instincts and savor the abundance of their own creativity.

Mirroring is an even more interactive style of brainstorming. Let's consider the well-known piano piece, Mozart's Rondo *alla turca* from the Sonata in A major, K. 331, excerpted in Example 13. Once the student has become comfortable with the notes, more musical vitality may still be needed. If so, I might invite him to come away from the piano and stand opposite me, poised and ready to move. I'd explain that I'm going to act out the piece a few different ways, in order to find out what I would like if I were playing it. His job is simply to mirror everything I do.

This piece is built on repeated modules of two bars or four bars. Dramatic contrasts from one module to the next make it entertaining and satisfying. But what sort of contrasts? Again, there are lots of choices. I can start section A quietly with held-back, suspenseful excitement and then have section B answer with jaunty aggressiveness. Or I can start A aggressively and change to witty and sly at B. I gesticulate and vocalize the passage several ways, hamming them up humorously and making sure the student matches my energy level as we mirror each other. I make sure

Example 13. Mozart, Rondo *alla turca* from Piano Sonata K. 331, beginning. Contrasting ideas A and B.

to cut myself off right in the middle of things and say off-handedly, "Well, that's one way, let's try something else," enjoying each style but not judging them or showing any attachment to a particular one. Then I quickly say, "Now it's your turn," and the student takes over as brainstormer. Only when we feel satisfied that our versions are lively and interesting do we go back to the instrument, taking turns playing while the other acts it out, swapping the lead back and forth, having fun with the material. Sometimes students are held back in this game by an overly reverential idea of Mozart, and need to hear down-to-earth assurances like, "Well, Mozart's been dead for centuries and I don't think he cares what we choose as long as it's interesting and reaches people." This, I believe, is substantially true.

Teachers may worry that brainstorming processes like this are too frivolous, not rigorous enough for musical masterpieces. But there is plenty of artistic integrity here, although that too requires some trust. It helps to remember that when you are brainstorming in any context (musical or not), the ground rule is to suspend judgment while ideas are generated and to trust in the wisdom of the final sorting-out process. In this way, the best musical ideas will emerge naturally. Inappropriate ones simply won't feel right, and useful ones will. And the good ideas will feel even more convincing for having come through the free-wheeling brainstorming process.

Be a student yourself

The normal setup of the studio lesson puts teachers on the sidelines much of the time, critiquing and making recommendations to the student. This can have the unfortunate effect of making teachers seem a bit too all-knowing. Sometimes well-meaning teachers exacerbate the situation by never being quite pleased in the lesson, always raising the bar just slightly (it's very easy for us to think that's what we're *supposed* to do). But how refreshing it would be for a student to walk in for a lesson and discover the teacher at the instrument, practicing a demanding passage, full of energy and gusto, making remarks like, "Wow, I'm still struggling with the fingering for this run—but I'll get it soon!" Why not show our feet of clay and engage in the very process we ask students to do? Extending this thought, it's highly desirable for teachers to memorize and perform too, if these are things they expect from students. Then everyone can compare notes about their experiences and learn more in the process. After all, would we seek out a tennis teacher who never plays tennis?

It's additionally convincing if the teacher is studying a skill other than music and is still a rookie at it: "My white-belt karate class is great, but it's been tough for me to memorize the forms" or "Will I ever master these Japanese phrases?" or "For some reason I had a frustrating singing lesson yesterday, but still I'm so excited to be studying voice." The message is clear: learning itself is a fulfilling adventure at all points in the process. In fact, psychologists have listed learning as one of the basic, universal joys of human experience.

Chapter 8

What is a lesson anyway?

The lesson is not a weekly examination. Students shouldn't have to prove their basic worth at each lesson. I have found it extremely helpful to say clearly, "I sense your natural musicality; you don't have to demonstrate that to me every week." I can see the relief in my students' eyes, which tells me how important it was for them to hear those words from me. (Wish I'd thought of it years ago!) Once they hear that basic acceptance, students find it much easier to relax and experiment with "un-lesson" strategies. People do need to feel understood and valued in order to learn.

Lessons do serve a good purpose as a checkpoint. Where are we in the process? Where might we go from here? How are things going? Here's a metaphor for lessons that students seem to respond to: think of a classical piece of music, with all its intricacy, as a complex machine with many moving parts. Your practice room is like a machine shop. There, you have an imaginary large sheet spread out on the floor, and you are sitting on the sheet with the components of the taken-apart machine all spread out around you. Occasionally you put the machine together and run it briefly to see how smoothly it goes; then you take it apart again so as to keep improving each component. You're in no hurry. Then you realize that it's the day of your lesson. You don't modify what you're doing, but just gather up the sheet with all the parts rolling around inside, sling it over your shoulder, and come to the lesson. Here you spread out the sheet on the floor and we take a look together at all the parts and discuss how you're working with them. "I'm using a number 4 oil on this gear," you might tell me, "and I spin it clockwise to make sure it moves freely." "Have you tried spinning it counterclockwise too?" I might ask. When it's time to put the machine together and run the whole thing, we will both sense that and will agree: next week you will perform this for me and we'll assess the results.

Whatever approach is used, teachers should make sure that students don't get ahead of themselves. Don't be willing to listen to half-baked, forced, tentative attempts to play the whole thing every week. With a new piece, as a rule of thumb, let at least three weeks of taken-apart "process" lessons go by before agreeing to give the machine a test run.

The more I ponder the dimensions of teaching, the more uneasy I feel at times about the word itself. *Teaching* seems to connote a one-way authoritarian setup, and even though that is totally appropriate and fine in some situations, too much teacherly advice can lead to student passivity, which is not so good. Is there a better word for teacher that doesn't sound too vague—such as consultant, facilitator, collaborator, resource?

Maybe the labels don't really matter as long as we're flexible about teaching and learning. It's satisfying to invent ways of structuring lessons that don't squelch student vitality. Lessons, or un-lessons, create an experience for two human beings, not just for the student. As I said at the outset of this chapter, that experience can be invigorating. This promise holds true for teachers and students alike.

9   The Un-Master Class
Rethinking a Tradition

Seventy people stood in a loose circle waiting for the workshop to begin. We had no idea what to expect. The leader, without a word, grabbed a large carton and dumped out its contents: more than a hundred yellow tennis balls, which started bouncing and skittering crazily around the spacious room. "Catch one and quickly find a partner!" cried the leader. "Now face each other at a distance of twenty-five feet or so and play catch, and when it's your turn to catch, close your eyes first!" Chaos and cheerful pandemonium ensued. Occasionally, though, with a surprised shout of exaltation, one of us did manage to catch a tennis ball somehow, even with our eyes closed.

The leader was Eloise Ristad, and this was my introduction to her work. A piano teacher from Boulder, Colorado, Eloise wasn't nearly as musically educated or proficient as many of her workshop clients were. But this turned out to be irrelevant, since Eloise had no intention of offering answers. She knew how to probe so that you could find your own answers.

Eloise was determined to bring exuberance, freshness, laughter, artistic honesty, and self-trust to musicians; she understood exactly what was needed. In her work she crossed boundaries that had rarely, if ever, been crossed before. People from all points on the spectrum of skill and experience participated equally in Eloise's work; veteran concert performers sought her out for artistic fine-tuning, young students and shaky amateurs hoped to overcome insecurities, and they all took part in the same groups. Violinists, saxophonists, pianists, opera singers, string quartets, jazz guitarists—musicians of all descriptions came together in the workshops and found fertile common ground.

Eloise modeled for me the idea that a purposeful performance class can have a strikingly different approach, philosophy, atmosphere, and sociology than the conventional master class. There can be a new role for the leader, and the attendees can function as far more than an audience; their pooled energy and insight provide a rich resource that can play a key role throughout the class.

In this chapter we look beyond our concerns about individual teachers and students working in the studio and practice room, and focus instead on musical work in groups. Group work can be uniquely energizing, freeing, and revelatory, and its possibilities are eliciting more and more interest among music teachers. More specifically, though, this chapter describes the performance workshop I have been offering since 1987, which I call The Un-Master Class.[1] A multifaceted group experience, the program seeks to maximize communicative vitality and authenticity in the art of performance and—as a corollary—self-trust and confidence for performers themselves. Experimental in nature, the class intertwines prepared performances (vocal and instrumental) with various group interactions based on body movement, dramatics, and other strategies that occur to us at the moment.

When skillfully conducted, a traditional master class can be of great value, both as instruction and inspiration. With this in mind I like to frame the Un-Master Class as a complement to master classes, an additional option for musicians who would like to come together for the purpose of improving their specific performances. After all, why can't we have several satisfying ways to collaborate, instead of always following the same structural model?

My development of the Un-Master Class had two main roots. One was my fulfilling childhood experience of Dalcroze Eurhythmics, with its body-centered approach to the essential energies of music (see chapter 1). The other was the direct inspiration of Eloise Ristad's work. But I was looking for a new performance-class format in the first place because I had mixed feelings about our prevailing institution for group instruction, the master class, and I was fascinated by what the alternatives might be.

The master class

A master class, like any other instructional mode, is exactly as effective or ineffective as the person conducting it. Master classes, which basically are music lessons given by a guest teacher in front of an audience, can be informative indeed. I have been privileged to see "masterful" classes that were fast moving, entertaining, enlightening, humane, flexible, energizing, and respectful of and interested in the student performer. But these attributes are somewhat rare, according my own experience and the reports of others.

Admittedly, the descriptions I offer here of master classes don't always paint the rosiest picture. But when I critique the role of the "maestro," for example, I'm doing so partly as a confession; I have engaged in many of the behaviors I describe, and I'm not especially proud of that fact. When I first found myself in a position to give master classes, I simply followed the models I'd seen, and—like most master class practitioners—I certainly meant well. Only later did I absorb the messages implicit in the wary eyes of students over the years. I began to grasp how I may have unwittingly disrespected them, and that there might be built-in problems with the time-honored master class format. These are the aspects I want to bring to light.

The format itself seems to invite a rather different outcome than the intended one: students frequently come away disheartened and (perhaps subtly) humiliated, having learned little of lasting value. It's ironic that the audience will sometimes feel quite pleased with a class in which the performing student herself ended up feeling frustrated, since it's the student who should matter most.

More than once I've heard from heartbroken teachers that their favorite advanced student, a sensitive and gifted soul, was made to feel so discredited, worthless, and embarrassed by a single master class experience that the student had quit playing music altogether. (Of course the guest "master" would have no way of knowing about such unintended consequences to his well-intended efforts.) On a personal note, I've observed a consistent reaction from fellow musicians when I tell them the somewhat provocative name of my workshops; when they hear the term "Un-Master" they usually chuckle mischievously and then confess that they eventually came to dread performing in conventional master classes. Clearly, then, many musicians find master classes questionable in some ways, and yet the tradition itself is rarely discussed.

With these thoughts in mind, let's take a closer look at that typical scenario and how it sometimes plays out. These descriptions are mostly composites from many different classes.

An audience assembles, comprised of music teachers and students in a specific performance discipline, such as voice, cello, or piano. Perhaps a few curious individuals from the general public have shown up as well. On some occasions the audience pays for the event; other times it is free. Prepared student performances are scheduled for the two-to-three-hour class. The guest "master" is introduced; this might be a famous performer in town to give a concert, an ex-performer, or a well-respected educator. The honored guest often makes a little introductory speech about how the world of interpretation is a wide one, there's no "best" way, and no one is obliged to follow whatever humble advice he may offer. The onlookers are usually in a happy mood of anticipation at the outset, intrigued by the possible drama of what will unfold and eager to glean illuminating trade secrets or artistic insights from the illustrious guest.

The first student is introduced. She hands the score to the maestro, takes her place onstage, and begins to perform. Usually she will be allowed to perform the piece all the way through. (I once saw a master class given by a legendary European soprano known for the obsessive artistic detail of her interpretations, and she startled the nervous young singer—and the audience—by stopping and correcting her after literally one word of the German art song ("Meine . . ." "STOP!"), thereby demolishing any self-confidence the student may have been trying to establish in the stressful situation. Fortunately, this is *not* typical.)

The student finishes the performance to a round of polite applause. Then maestro comes over, perhaps pats her on the back, and says smilingly, "Congratulations—what a nice job," but if the student is a master class veteran she is not taken in at all by this sweetness, as evidenced by her stony facial expression; she knows exactly what is to come and is bracing for it. Maestro continues magnanimously, "Now there are just a few little things I'm wondering about" and pulls up a chair so they can share thoughts more closely.

But it doesn't turn out to be sharing or a dialogue at all. Oftentimes, after a forty-five-minute teaching segment, onlookers will realize that they have not heard a single word from the student. Part of the built-in ambiguity here is that a master class is indeed a performance, and there is an audience that (rightly) expects to be played to in some way. The maestro is usually someone who is quite used to the stage, knowing how to exude charisma and make audiences love him. He (rightly) directs a good portion of his remarks out to the audience, generalizing from the case at hand for everyone's edification and perhaps cracking a few jokes. All of this, however, can make the student performer feel almost irrelevant to the proceedings, even as her presentation of the music is dissected and analyzed like a specimen on a microscope slide.

A half hour goes by, and torpor begins to set in. Somehow we haven't gotten past the first eight measures, endlessly repeated, evaluated, and polished. The audience is shifting restlessly or nodding off from time to time. The maestro, though, is getting more and more musically enthused and insistent, because his own artistic juices are flowing, and he really intends to make a difference in that student and get her to emulate his own performance instincts. By this point she can't play a single note or phrase without being interrupted, commented upon, and remade in maestro's image.

But what can a person really learn from someone else's instincts? Sometimes not much, especially if it's a musical situation where any two performing artists might make quite different (and equally valid) interpretive choices. Instincts work for one person but may seem totally arbitrary to another. I thought of this recently as I watched a distinguished, elderly pianist becoming more and more directive and agitated as he coached a student in a Rachmaninoff concerto (he had started out quite relaxed and genial). "No!" he kept shouting, pacing back and forth and clapping out the time aggressively, "don't bend the tempo at all! Get where you're going! Don't be so self-indulgent—play each phrase straightforwardly, just like Rachmaninoff did!" When he finally got her to follow his lead, he relented just a bit and admitted grudgingly, "Now you are *beginning* to sound like a pianist." The audience, momentarily roused by the violence of his outbursts (which were a bit comical and probably deliberately so, since he was a crafty and rather hammy performer at heart), smiled and nodded in agreement. They were solidly on the maestro's side in this, even if he was acting a bit autocratic for the moment; apparently that just showed how much he cared about the music and bringing it to life. He was certainly convincing. The student, understandably, continued to look impassive; it's not pleasant to be publicly told, in effect, that your own choices deserved ridicule and were so wrong-headed that they couldn't even be considered those of "a pianist."

While I watched, I daydreamed about rewinding the scene and replaying it with a radically different script, one that gives exactly the opposite advice about the music. This was easy to imagine, since I had indeed heard the opposite view expressed many times in other master classes and performances, and just as convincingly. "No!" shouts the maestro in my imagination, "don't play rigidly in tempo like a heartless robot! You're the soloist in a romantic concerto! Linger, smell the roses! Don't you know that you must make love to every phrase in Rachmaninoff?" Once again, the audience smiles and nods as the stoic student swallows her humiliation.

Experienced students are aware that there's no way to predict which of their choices might be held up to ridicule in a master class, or why. It's disorienting to find the ground shifting under one in such a way, to never know what to expect from authority figures; psychologists ascribe the chronic insecurities of the children of alcoholic parents to a similar dynamic. Musicians finding themselves exposed to this interpretive mine-field tend to retreat, play it safe, and thus lose commitment and vitality. This is ironic, because the courage of their own convictions is often all that they need as performers. I was delighted to hear one insightful maestro say to a student, "That's not the usual texture for Rachmaninoff, and I would never play it quite the way you do, but it's very special and seems to suit you, so I wouldn't change a thing!" Most of the time, though, if the playing is unconvincing, the maestro will move in and take charge of the interpretation—perhaps mostly for the audience's sake, to keep the class moving along.

Oftentimes a performance just seems lacking somehow, even though all the details are in place. In that instance an honest listener's reaction might be, "It's not coming across to me, but I'm not exactly sure why." An exploratory process (which would take a bit of time) might then reveal a good, authentic solution. But does a vague statement that expresses uncertainty sound worthy of a guest maestro? Not according to our mental prototype of a master class, which expects more omniscience in the teacher role. This flaw in the master class tradition has led to a primary goal of the Un-Master Class: to be able to say as a point of departure, "Your performance needs something, but we're not sure what," thus respecting the student's right to find an individual interpretation that works but without resorting to preemptive quick fixes from others. This is a substantively different problem-solving route from many (but not all) master classes.

The master class tradition is a long one, going back to the group lessons taught by Liszt and other revered European pedagogues in the nineteenth century, many of whom were indeed abrupt, temperamental, and disrespectful of students (as chronicled by Amy Fay and others). Hollywood movies have further entrenched the colorful stereotype of the brilliant, haughty, and dismissive virtuoso-teacher, so we've come to expect this demeanor to a degree. While teaching styles have generally softened and become more humane in recent years, I worry that certain underlying traits of the classes have not changed; for example, focusing on the negative and not explicitly acknowledging what is good. While this may be the exception rather than the rule, I once overheard a master class leader muttering to herself after the student performance, "His rhythm was good, so we won't need to mention that." But how would it hurt a student to have his admirable rhythm praised in front of an audience? This presenter, who was actually quite charming and likeable, clearly felt that her mission was solely to critique: to point out flaws and try to find remedies.

Subtle (probably unconscious) disrespect of students can take many forms, including jokes at the student's expense and unflattering mimicry in order to make a musical point. In a high-profile master class a talented fourteen-year-old pianist performed his Chopin waltz. "Well now, what do you think a Chopin waltz is really about?" the famous maestro asked him slyly, having acknowledged nothing about the polished performance the boy had just given. When the boy couldn't find an answer (who could under those conditions?), the maestro ended the suspense triumphantly, with a twinkle in his eye: "Seduction and sex, that's what every note is about!" Titters from the audience, helpless blushes from the understandably mortified fourteen-year-old. Moments like this exemplify the point made by *The New York Times* music critic Bernard Holland, "It is the students who play and sing, but make no mistake, it is the masters of these master classes who are 'on.' The audience rules. Every role is played out for its benefit."[2]

Mimicry of a student takes place not only in master classes but in private lessons too; like everything else, though, its effect—shame—is heightened in the public arena of a master class. This is a tricky issue for teachers, because mimicking a student can be a highly effective form of pedagogy; it makes a musical point instantaneously, saving a lot of time and a lot of talking. Music speaks its own language, and words can never quite capture what a direct musical illustration can. So it's educationally efficient to tell someone, "You're doing it like this" (mimicry of student), "but why not do it like this?" (acting out a better way). The point will be clear right away. Unfortunately it's almost impossible not to exaggerate the mimicry a bit in order to nail down the point; for example, "Those repeated notes are all sounding alike" (comically slouching pantomime of tedious, heavy beats, idiotic facial expression)—"why not shape them like so?" (aristocratic bearing, eloquent lyric gestures). The student understands immediately, but this morsel of valid learning is ingested with a bitter coating of mockery, which adds to the student's shame and self-doubt, especially when the scene is played out in front of a chuckling, delighted audience. Even if the mimicry is done good-humoredly, or with a tossed-aside disclaimer like "Of course I'm exaggerating," the effect of humiliation is not much lessened.

Quite often the maestro goes one step further and illustrates the musical point by performing the passage in question. Again, there is educational clarity but sometimes at the expense of the student's dignity, since the student has no choice but to stand by in an appreciative attitude while her playing is made to look rather pitiful by comparison. Maestros tend to play quite beautifully in these situations too, because it's easy to perform a short snippet publicly when there is no pressure, and one can always ensure that there's no pressure by tossing off remarks like "I haven't touched this in thirty years" or "Forgive me if I have to sight-read." Such statements only make the audience even more impressed with the maestro's sophisticated playing, again at the subtle expense of the student. To quote Bernard Holland again, the master class "is more about the teacher than the taught, [and] its format assures that even with the best of intentions the student is the least important element involved."

The Artist Within: a workshop and its legacy

At times each of us needs another person to open a new door, to show us how different things can be. This was Eloise Ristad's role in my life, as it was for many other people she met. Her special talent was in helping others find ways to encounter and communicate their resourceful inner selves; she freed them from the prison of their own self-consciousness. Those who knew her well considered her to be, most basically, an intuitive healer. She believed that playful, even seemingly ridiculous, interactions between people could have integrity and could clear the way for authentic artistry to emerge. She got results because of her pure belief that there was indeed a unique artist within each person.

Several features of Eloise's classes, which she called The Artist Within, have influenced my work directly and undoubtedly the work of others as well. Perhaps she, in her turn, was inspired by others and adapted their techniques, at least to a degree. At any rate, her classes had the justified reputation of being unique; some of their specific practices, summarized here, present a clear alternative to those of the traditional master class.

WARM UP THE GROUP FIRST

All attendees—performers and listeners alike—are invited to be involved and lend their energy to the proceedings. The class is not a star turn for the presenter or a show offered to a passive audience. In order to loosen up the atmosphere, dissolve barriers, and activate group energy and insight, the class needs structured activities and interactions for everyone before the performances take place.

EMBODY THE MUSIC

Avoid the familiar realm of verbal discussion and advice-giving. Assume that all people can move and vocalize creatively and expressively. Assume that the musical language of movement and sound is more precise than that of words. Get instrumentalists away from their instruments; they may be

> *The musical language of movement and sound is more precise than that of words*

hiding behind them. Show them how revealing it can be to perform a violin sonata without a violin, how much that can clarify about one's fundamental intentions and relationship to the music.

JOIN THE PERFORMER

It may be a bit embarrassing to try to perform a violin sonata without a violin the first time, but it will feel a lot safer if others join you in that activity, unquestioningly mirroring your every gesture and sound. When we're all doing it together, we energize each other and there's no one left behind to play the critic. Performers in master classes tend to feel isolated and constantly judged; this is a central drawback of the format. But for performers to shed passivity and explore their own artistic solutions, they need an environment that is comfortable, fertile, and responsive. Ideas themselves evolve and develop, instead of remaining fixed, when they are faithfully shared, mirrored without comment.

This approach is strikingly similar to the style of psychotherapy personified by Carl Rogers (1902–1987). In Rogers's famously empathetic approach, the therapist in effect "joins" the client instead of sitting back and giving advice. The client's own inner wisdom is respected and trusted and the therapist functions merely as a prism or catalyst. The belief is that if clients are listened to actively and with both acceptance and caring, their self-acceptance will blossom, causing their thoughts to open, become unstuck, and flow toward a personally authentic solution to the problem at hand.

BRAINSTORM

Generate lots of ideas, in the faith that the best ones will naturally come to the fore since the group will immediately sense their worth. This is a great advantage of activating a group: its collective wisdom. Take full advantage of the presence of a participating group to try new things and expand your creativity, all in the protected context of brainstorming, in which possibilities are never censored while they are in the process of being generated. Epitomize through brainstorming the philosophy that musical truth is an ongoing, open-ended quest. Eloise was remarkably pure in her trust in this process, her refusal to pollute it through ego—much like a Rogerian psychotherapist. Even if a particular exploration yielded an unexpectedly stunning result, she remained neutral (while the rest of the group erupted in cheers); it simply didn't matter if she was pleased or not, nor was she about to claim gleeful ownership of the victory as we teachers often do ("See how dramatically that improved, now that you followed my excellent advice?"). All that mattered was the performer and the audience and the authenticity of what passed between them.

Require that all performers think about, and then declare, their stake in the performance: in other words, get them to say what they want. This can be done by asking such open questions as

- What's the main thing you'd like to know about how you perform this?
- What do you hope will happen for the audience when you break the silence and play these specific notes? If we paid for tickets, would we get our money's worth? Why?
- What do you really think of this piece? Did you choose it, or did someone else? Do you love it? If so, how would you describe to someone who's never heard it what makes it special?
- Is there anything you worry about when you are performing this?

Thanks to the group warm-up, which relaxes people and opens up their trust, the answers tend to be honest, individual, and surprising. Of course, the very fact that such questions are being asked makes clear an underlying philosophy: everyone who steps in front of others to create a musical performance must have some personal stake in what happens. In a way, this stands the master class on its head as the usual passivity and guardedness of performers disappear. Eloise invited a collaborative effort. What she really wanted to know from the performer was: What sort of feedback do *you* want—how can we best help you?

As a way of illustrating how Eloise's techniques could cause a person to encounter himself in a fresh way, let me offer a personal story. In one session with her, I was working on a prelude by J. S. Bach. The piece was fairly new to me; I had learned the notes but was still experimenting with the interpretation. With

Bach's music, so pure on the page and unencumbered by expressive indications from the composer, I like to let the interpretation emerge from the notes, evolve naturally over time. I was away from the piano, dancing the music while Eloise mirrored my moves; this was a stately piece in a minor key, filled with rather dignified dotted-note figures. After a short time I stopped, saying, "I can feel how nondescript and generalized my dancing is—I'm even boring myself!" Eloise seemed interested in my comment but offered no guidance. We thought about this for a long moment. Then I heard myself blurt out, "Well, I may not know where I'm going with this yet, but I can tell you exactly how I *don't* want to play it!"

"Oh?" asked Eloise, more intrigued. "Oh, yeah," said I, warming to my subject with spirit, "I've always hated it when people play baroque music in that really pompous, self-important way, you know—sort of flinging their hair around on every dotted rhythm," and I proceeded to offer a humorous pantomime of such obnoxious performances. Eloise grinned appreciatively, and I should have known what was to come next. "Well, since you're not sure what you want yet," she suggested, "why not dance what you *don't* want—this egotistical style that irks you so much?" Which I did, with Eloise again mirroring me without comment.

It took only a few of these "pompous" dance steps for me to grasp what was happening. I realized:

- I seem to know exactly how to do the "pompous" movement.
- It's energizing, fun to do, and I'm enjoying it.
- It seems to fit the music perfectly.
- So what's this issue I have about being pompous?

Artistry should transcend one's own idiosyncratic personality, yet I had been unwittingly limiting myself through old habits of thought. After all, "pompous" is just a word—and what's wrong with a piece of music being pompous anyway? Eloise's interaction with me certainly wasn't teaching or coaching in any conventional sense, but it offered me insight and artistic liberation—freedom from myself—in a way that conventional teaching never had.

The Un-Master Class

Why the term "Un-Master"? It captures several features of the workshop, which distinguish the session from master classes in key ways:

A DIFFERENT ROLE FOR THE LEADER: catalyst, facilitator, not an omniscient teacher

A DIFFERENT ROLE FOR THE ATTENDEES: participatory, not passive; joining together to furnish group reactions and insights

A DIFFERENT POPULATION: any performing category, not restricted to one genre

A DIFFERENT FORMAT: flexible, interspersing group activities with performances.

Students take the lead in an Un-Master Class exercise. PHOTO BY REBECCA COONEY

While the underlying philosophy of the Un-Master Class is fundamentally consistent with that of Eloise Ristad's workshops, certain aspects differ. Perhaps most significant is the incorporation of techniques and concepts from Dalcroze Eurhythmics, notably in the warm-up phase. The overall sequence and musical structure of the warm-up are original as well, and many of the interactive strategies for performer and group are of my own devising.

Throughout the ongoing process of developing the Un-Master Class, I've found that it has taken lots of experimentation (juicy mistakes!) to come up with format ideas that work well and that seem to suit me. And I'm gratified to say that there have been some exciting breakthrough moments for participants. What I offer here are only a few of the limitless possibilities that exist once we let our creativity roam past the known boundaries of the master class; surely there are many ways in which performance classes might evolve.

Un-Master Class techniques for working with performers can't be listed as a standardized formula; they arise from the situation and the imagination of everyone present. We do follow the general principles of Eloise Ristad's work: eliciting a focus from the performer, brainstorming solutions instead of giving advice, finding ways to physicalize the music together with the performer. For those readers who might want to try out the techniques with a group, I will provide a rather detailed description of the basic program and its concepts in this chapter.

But before going further, I should mention a key consideration to keep in mind with workshops of this type: as with any process that asks for direct physical participation (something the attendees may not have known about in advance), we must respect the reluctance that some individuals might have. When I explain a few of the workshop's principles at the outset of the session, I invite participants to take part rather than pressure them to do so; they may have personal reasons not to join in, which, though often unspoken, are valid and important to them.

There are practical issues to consider as well. The class can succeed with almost any size group of about eight to about twenty-five. Larger numbers are fine too, but people may have to take turns participating in some of the activities, or some may simply observe. The population might consist of an existing music theory class, or a music teachers' association, conservatory students, adult recreational musicians, or any ad hoc group. They can be all one genre of performer or mixed. I prefer to work with people no younger than high school age, but oftentimes younger students work out extremely well if they are responsive, curious, and not too self-conscious. Participants are encouraged to wear comfortable clothing.

Because there will be plenty of activity, the Un-Master Class needs a generous amount of space, with movable chairs if possible. Picture twenty people standing in a circle at arm's-length distance from each other, and you get a rough idea of what's needed. Examples of good spaces: a classroom, a choir room, a rehearsal hall, a stage, or a very large den.

Some equipment also should be in place: a good piano, of course, and a few music stands if ensembles might perform, as well as recorded music for the exercises (as explained in the next section) and playback equipment with speakers large enough for the music to sound stirring and inspiring. Finally, you'll need a few objects that can be passed from hand to hand, such as footbags (Hacky Sacks), beanbags, stress balls, or tennis balls. It's best if the objects aren't able to bounce, roll away, or fly out of control; that's why some sort of beanbag is ideal.

An Un-Master Class has two fundamental components: group activities and performances.

GROUP ACTIVITIES

The activities at the start of the class, which may take up to half an hour, are intended to loosen us up, energize us, bond the group together in some ways, and remind us what it's like to share the pure joy of letting music course through our bodies and activate every part of us. They are designed to transform the usual classroom atmosphere—somewhat guarded and passive—into a freer one which will be fertile for the class's experimental and participatory nature: an atmosphere of trust of music itself, of other people, and of our own impulses. The activities also familiarize the group quickly with specific techniques that will prove useful once the performances begin.

For all these reasons the introductory activities must never be rushed; establishing an atmosphere takes its own time and is well worth the commitment. We also need to give participants enough time to get past any anxiety about doing new things; understandably there may be some nervous laughter and chatter at the start. Since most of the spontaneous reacting we are about to do is quite natural to any two-year-old, the challenge here is not about teaching anything new *per se* but more about social behavior. Can grown-ups shed their reserve and give in to the moment? That's what we'd like to explore.

Needless to say, a string quartet sitting there at the start of class with their instruments out, all warmed up, tuned, and ready to play, may be taken aback when told that no one is going to play a note for the next thirty minutes, but they usually adjust quickly once the exercises start.

To supply accompaniment for the activities, we must be ready with some really good recorded music and high-quality playback equipment. The more vivid the sound, the more the music can sweep the group along and help people to forget themselves in the activities. Customizing the recorded music is a nice way to make the class one's own. Since there is no limit to the musical choices one could make, I'll describe useful categories as opposed to listing specific pieces. It works well to make separate tapes for these categories, creating a sort of flexible tool kit that will be useful in whatever combinations may seem most appropriate at any moment. These categories don't have (or need to have) strict definitions or boundaries; effective choices may blend two or more categories. Categories of recorded music for the class may include:

> VARIETY: entertaining, attractive, high-energy music, full of changes in mood, tempo, texture, and dynamics. Lots to respond to. Avoid predictable, regular tempos, except for brief periods. Unfamiliar works work especially well—the response is purer. Make the tape funny and riveting by cutting off one piece very abruptly and continuing with something totally different in feel. Examples: symphonic works or tone-poems by Tchaikovsky, Dvořák; overtures like that of Strauss's *Die Fledermaus*, a Bartók string quartet, a perky bluegrass tune, a rhapsodic work like a Russian piano concerto, tribal drumming, an opera aria, Vivaldi's *Four Seasons*

> CALM MIRRORING: something slow, otherworldly, and unpredictable like Gregorian chant or traditional Asian flute music

> BIZARRE GROUP MOVEMENT: music with a dark, threatening, volatile mood and highly kinetic, primal atmosphere. Examples: electronic music or modernistic science-fiction movie scores, or something like Stravinsky's *Rite of Spring* or Berg's *Wozzeck*

> CALM-SPIRITUAL GROUP MOVEMENT: any heartfelt adagio, such as the *Air on the G String* from Bach's Orchestral Suite No. 3 or the Barber *Adagio for Strings*.

Before the activities begin, it is important to have a minute or two of general warm-up. The goal here is simply to energize ourselves, loosen up, get blood flowing. This part needn't be structured; leaders should do whatever suits them. Make sure people stretch, jump around, use their voices, and activate their lower limbs (musicians are often a bit sedentary). As leader I can make it easy for the others by doing something first and having them copy me. People are liberated by this, because it takes all responsibility away from them: if the group ends up doing something wild and ridiculous, that was *my* idea; they are not to blame! This type of leadership (willingness to make fools of ourselves first) is the key to success for the entire activity portion of the Un-Master Class.

Call and Response. Now to put the principles into practice. The most basic goal (I might remind the group) is to give our critical minds a rest and awaken our natural enjoyment of responding immediately and fully to a musical stimulus, just as we all did at the age of two or three. For this, there's no need to invent a new technique; the handiest one has been used in countless cultures all over the world for centuries: Call and Response.

First get a good four-beat rhythm going. I use a tape of African drumming or ask some group members to drum out a jazzy, infectious four-beat on whatever is handy.

I then "call" by clapping out a rhythmic pattern that occupies four beats; the group "responds" by immediately clapping it back to me. I try to make it lively, with colorful dynamics, choreography, even facial expressions. I insist that the group capture all the energy and character I've put into it, and I do not accept listless or all-purpose efforts on their part. They need to give themselves wholeheartedly to this simple exercise.

After several clapping patterns, I surprise them by doing vocal cries, big body gestures, thigh-slaps, anything at all that can take place in four beats, and the more silly and outrageous the better. If this goes well, some individuals in the group may want to try giving the "call." Then we can start to vary things even more, by changing the rhythm sometimes to two beats or eight beats, or shifting suddenly from something soft and whispery to something loud and startling. Surprise is good; anything that causes laughter is good because it's freeing. Games like this create instant energy.

Passing the Ball. Now the group is ready for Passing the Ball, which is fundamentally a Dalcroze game. Again, instead of an actual ball it's good to use something like a beanbag that won't bounce or roll away. The object should be passed from hand to hand, never thrown. This game uses a "variety" tape, one with lots of hard-to-predict musical changes. Everyone stands in a large circle, arm's-length apart. We pass the "ball" around with the idea that it can tell the story of the music, in all its variety. The ball or beanbag inscribes phrases in the air, explores the space around the person, reflects just how the music feels at that moment. People shouldn't plan what they're going to do—the music must make them do it at the moment. They should be invited to move their feet, as long as we don't call it dancing because then they'll get shy about it.

The moment of passing to the next person is crucial. It's best to do it on the beat, if possible, although I wouldn't make too big an issue of this. Many times, I've observed, people create freely expressive shapes with the ball, but then all the energy (and music) goes out of them when they have to pass the ball to the next person; this they do in a listless, neutral way. I take this to mean that they're still self-conscious, trapped in their own space, and shy about imposing, actually sharing music with another human being. So I show them how it feels to really pass the ball right—to slap it into someone's hand when the music is aggressive, drop it in as lightly as a feather when the music is *dolcissimo.* This takes some assertive leadership; to literally "bestow" musical expression on another person is an essential way to dissolve barriers in the class, and sometimes participants need a little push in the direction of that enjoyable connection with others.

We start three or four balls around and then change the game so that the ball is passed not to the next person but to someone on the opposite side of the large circle. Take the ball to them "in the music," pass it, and then take their place in the circle. The watchwords through all this activity are: Match the energy of the music! I've found that people tend to be a bit reluctant to interact and stay focused, but will respond well to enthusiastic exhortations by the leader. It helps that this game is not only high-energy but rather chaotic; people seem to find that comical, and it frees them up more.

Mirroring in Pairs. This next exercise has a calming effect. People should arrange themselves in groups of two, face each other squarely, relax their bodies, and gaze into each other's eyes without any expression. They should have plenty of room around them. There will be lots of talking and laughter at first, but it needs to die away, because the rule here is: No talking. This exercise explores the penetrating language of gesture, and talking will simply neutralize the effect, allowing us to revert to our everyday social selves. I use a tape of the "calm mirroring" type.

Each duo designates a leader and a follower, with the understanding that this is only temporary, since the lead will shift from person to person. The instructions are that when the music starts, the "leader" moves however he or she feels at the moment, and the "follower" will mirror those movements simultaneously while they both maintain eye contact. It doesn't matter what anyone else in the room is doing. When they hear the instruction "Change!" the lead must shift seamlessly to the other person in the duo. Surprise the group by stopping the tape and making them change partners frequently. This is a good ice-breaker for the group, as it asks (in a fairly safe way) for some real expressive intimacy between persons, often strangers. For this reason, the eye contact is often difficult for people to maintain, but if they can manage it the activity will be more effective in helping them open up and build trust. This is the same sort of wordless intimacy we experience in a good musical performance.

The mirroring exercise: exploring immediacy and trust. PHOTO BY
ARTIE LIMMER

Having established some expressive comfort and freedom in the
group, we can now begin to stretch ourselves expressively. We are
ready to move past social politeness into a more primal zone of
feeling, which is the fabric of music's beauty and power. I like to
use a "bizarre group movement" tape here—something angular,
spooky, and dark. The group re-forms into a large circle, with the
leader in the center. When the music starts, the leader improvises
movement while everyone mirrors it simultaneously. Then, in
character, the leader wends his way out to the circle and tacitly
indicates that the lead is being passed to someone else by taking
that person's place. The new person, now in the middle of the circle, has control of the game and of the musical expression. The
lead is thus passed to everyone eventually. As before, everyone
should match the music's energy and stay in character at the
moment of transfer to another person.

Chapter 9

The entire group mirrors the movement. PHOTO BY REBECCA COONEY

Many have reported that although at first they feared being in
the middle, once they got there they felt surprisingly safe, commanding, and "understood" by the group. This is a key point of the
exercise. If some participants still have a polite, all-purpose, pleasant smile on their faces throughout this part, you know that they
are resisting the music's force; others, however, will kick off their
shoes and plunge in eagerly with pantherlike intensity, as if they'd
been waiting for this chance for years. It is humbling for the leader
to notice how unpredictable such reactions can be; those with
flamboyant social personas may be reticent, while mousier types
may electrify the room in dynamic Martha Graham style. People
are revealing another level of who they are, and extending that
to others.

To round out the initial activity portion, I change to the
"calm-spiritual group movement" music while continuing the pre-
vious exercise. Although the format is the same, the music is now

more ceremonial and healing, which helps the group to bond a bit more. By this time, laughter and other forms of deflection have usually died down, demonstrating participants' respect for each other and for the direction we are all moving in together.

PERFORMANCES

Finally it's time to pick up the instruments. I summarize for everyone the point we've come to. The activities have primed the group for performance in a special way; we've been listening with our whole bodies, enjoying an immediate response to music. We've also practiced some simple communication techniques that will become useful as we proceed—passing the ball to music, mirroring someone else's movements and sounds, sharing our energy. Therefore we must take care with the transition as we take seats and prepare to listen; we don't want our receptivity to evaporate, nor is this the occasion for intellectualizing or received ideas like "Don't use much pedal in Mozart." All we care about is what's happening right now.

Based on the preliminary dialogue with the performer, the leader offers some specific focus for the group to keep in mind during the performance, and during the verbal feedback that will follow it. Examples: "John is worried that this sensitive slow piece will become boring" or "Jane wants to know if this music tells a dramatic story." It's even better if the group can be given a specific assignment, such as reporting any mood-adjectives that pop into their heads while listening, or noticing if one section is more effective than another.

Here's What I Got. After the performance, I model for the class the type of verbal feedback I want, then invite others to join in. There is a ground rule for comments: we want honest statements that offer a reaction in clear, descriptive terms but that *do not* take the form of actual suggestions. I summarize this verbal feedback as Here's What I Got. These can be general or specific "I-statements" but should never cross the line into Why Don't You Try This? (or its more subtle, tactful version, Wouldn't It Be Even More Effective If You Did This?). All we're doing is holding up a realistic mirror to the performer, which the trusting atmosphere created by the activities makes possible. What we're not doing is preempting the performer's own chance to respond to the feedback. Consider these examples of Here's What I Got:

- I felt carried away to a land of dreams from the very first note.
- I was bored for most of it, but the forceful ending got my attention.
- I sensed that you were straining in the fast parts, but your flair excited me.

From such exchanges with the performer, a focus for improvement will usually emerge. Occasionally, though, if the performance fulfills the stated agenda wonderfully, the feedback will be purely celebratory—and every performer can certainly use such affirmation once in a while! It keeps us going.

But let's say we have indeed pinpointed an area for improvement. Perhaps the expressive content seems nondescript for some reason. Here are some techniques that will then put the group to good use.

- Performer "plays" the piece with no instrument, just gesticulations and sounds. A handful of other participants mirror this. Try it three different ways. Don't judge them. How did they feel? If some especially vital results do emerge, how do they compare with the energy we got from the actual playing? The findings here can be quite surprising. If the performer comes up with something new that everyone responds to, he should immediately take that energy back to the instrument and see what comes out.

- Group forms a circle around the player and his instrument and passes the ball as he plays, reflecting his playing as closely as possible; the player watches this and responds, seeing his nuances immediately embodied by the whole group. Does every measure feel the same? Does the ebb and flow feel right physically to the group? Encourage the player to experiment with some daring new choices.
- Group does mirrored movement to the live music. It's fascinating (and revealing) to watch others embody the notes that we play. Encourage the movements and the performance to influence each other.

Embodying the performer's phrasing. PHOTO BY REBECCA COONEY

- Space the group around the room in clusters; have the performer deliver one phrase right to the faces of the people in one cluster, then dash impulsively to another cluster to deliver the next musical thought. Were the musical statements immediate? Were they convincing? Were they alive?

199

Chapter 9

The answers will come from the pooled awareness of everyone present. When an Un-Master Class works well, the class becomes the master. People trust their perceptions, both as individuals and as a group. They find artistic rigor within themselves, not in deference to an outside "expert." They demonstrate belief in each other, and interact with more spontaneity. And when the class is over, they linger and talk together with unusual openness about their performing experiences, their struggles, and their dreams.

10 | *Adventurous Amateurs*

What do Sherlock Holmes and Albert Einstein have in common?

Both were extraordinary thinkers, one a fictional genius, the other a real genius—curious, original, and brilliant. And both were amateur violinists. The link between these aspects is significant: when either man got really stuck in his problem solving, he would turn to the same remedy: playing the violin.

A typical scene in the detective novel finds Dr. Watson, the loyal assistant, trudging up the stairs—knowing, from the wild violin sounds he heard, that the great Sherlock Holmes's powers of logical deduction were being sorely tested by the case at hand. In one story Watson observed, "Sometimes the chords were sonorous and melancholy. Occasionally they were fantastic and cheerful. Clearly they reflected the thoughts which possessed him, but whether the music aided those thoughts . . . was more than I could determine."[1]

Holmes apparently trusted the process of logical deduction, but he trusted another process too—the physical, absorbing act of music making. The two processes interacted somehow, one enhancing the other in a way that the author hints at but doesn't attempt to define.

Einstein also found a way to facilitate his thinking through violin playing. He may not have been an especially skilled violinist, but that is clearly not relevant. As one biographer relates:

> He had his music. But this, as he would explain on occasions, was in some ways an extension of his thinking processes, a method of allowing the subconscious to solve

particularly tricky problems. "Whenever he felt that he had come to the end of the road or into a difficult situation in his work," his elder son has said, "he would take refuge in music, and that would usually resolve all his difficulties."[2]

Musical forms, struggles, beauty, and physical patterns took both these legendary minds beyond the conventional—into an advanced type of metaphoric thought. In both cases their result-fixated minds eased up somehow, "allowing the subconscious" to lead the way—and musical performance provided this fruitful link between conscious and subconscious.

In short, they solved real-world problems by losing themselves in music, specifically in the physicality of the violin. I would guess that Einstein was not a timid or cautious player, either. He attributed his scientific creativity directly to this quality of childlike inquisitiveness, a plunge-right-in approach to his environment that I call physical intuition. And Einstein often said that his most famous theory was also inspired by music, its forms and relationships.

It seems that certain physical actions fire the brain, create connections, and accelerate thought. We have all had the experience of being literally unable to sit still when we are on the verge of resolving something in our minds. We pace up and down or jiggle a leg, almost as if such involuntary motions were needed to propel our thoughts forward. Sometimes the mind-body dynamic works a bit differently: while taking a long walk or rowing the boat across the lake, just letting our thoughts drift, we suddenly receive from the unconscious—with effortless ease—the solution to a conundrum that had been vexing us for weeks. I can testify that playing the piano has this effect; maybe it has something to do with both sides of the brain being stimulated by the independent articulations of both hands, and at the same time both

> *Certain physical actions fire the brain, create connections, and accelerate thought.*

sides communicating and integrating with each other. In any event, I have to keep a notepad handy while practicing, because I tend to get all kinds of unbidden information ranging from the trivial (where I left the car keys) to the momentous (my life goal for the next decade).

This fertile mind-body unity is only one of the riches to be found in making music—at any level—as an adult. Ironically, far too many adults, even if they do take the initiative to start or return to music study, are so modest in their expectations that these rewards turn out to be only a fraction of what they might have been.

An essay in *The New York Times Magazine* illustrated this point. Entitled "A Joyful Noise—How to Practice Without Hope of Perfection," it chronicled the feelings of an adult writer taking piano lessons for the first time at an urban music conservatory.

> And so it began—an excruciating half-hour of mistakes, confusion, and deep, deep frustration. I've never been more relieved to exit a room in my life. As I turned to sprint down the stairs and back across the street to safety, the door of the practice room across from mine opened and a small boy came out—a small boy with a stack of complicated sonatas and concertos as thick as a phone book. The humiliation was complete.
>
> The weeks staggered by. I dreaded going to lessons when I hadn't made any progress. . . . I practiced dutifully at the conservatory every night for an hour, though the only thing I could hear clearly was poor Bach rolling in his grave.[3]

Apparently, judging by the next week's letters to the editor, these charmingly candid confessions struck home with other readers. I believe the writer spoke for many as she expressed her awe of young talent, her resigned acceptance of slow and doubtful progress, and her guilt at mangling sublime music like that of Bach.

The paradox is that adult music learners, while they often have the lowest expectations, are in a uniquely excellent position to succeed. Many come to this endeavor with fervent desire, love of music, enchantment with the idea of making music with their own bodies and emotions, and leisure time and disposable income to support the lessons. Even more important, they bring maturity and intelligence to the project. But how much can adults learn if they are constantly comparing themselves negatively to others (children, no less) and feeling guilty about every unmusical wrong note? Add to this the pervasive notion of practice as tedious discipline, adherence to the traditional "no-mistakes" philosophy, and uncertainty that they have any real talent for music, and they soon find themselves in a state of semi-paralysis of body and mind.

Let's contrast music study with golf, another favorite self-improvement undertaking of mature individuals. Golf is challenging and unpredictable, just like music performance. Happily, though, golf isn't generally played by precocious kids; therefore, no need for self-deprecating comparisons to little prodigies. A botched golf swing is silent and (if no one happens to be looking) unobserved by anyone. An obvious musical clinker, though, resonates embarrassingly through the house; even the neighbors are often subjected to it. And while golf may be a beautiful game, it has no equivalent of a Bach or a Mozart whose divine legacy we run the risk of desecrating; therefore, no aesthetic guilt.

Golf is also widely valued as a personal journey, an absorbing, enriching, ongoing challenge of self-mastery in which struggle is expected, even embraced. Accuracy and control are rare, and if they do happen occasionally the golfer feels triumphant. Golfers, in other words, are philosophical.

But adults at the piano, or any other instrument, are often disconcerted by how much they feel like children; the situation itself seems to evoke this reaction. Wayne Booth, a professor emeritus of English at the University of Chicago who took up the cello as an adult, puzzled about his shamed bumbling whenever a chamber music colleague made a polite suggestion that he turn a particular phrase more musically:

> I try it—but my embarrassment makes me play it even worse. . . . It would no doubt shock her if she discovered how the little boy in me cringes over those failures. It shocks me. So I usually try to conceal how much feeling of a nonmusical kind has gone into my unimpressive phrasings: anxiety, tension, a sense of inadequacy.[4]

Even the word *amateur* has built-in conflicts of meaning, and I've wrestled with that in the writing of this book. While it literally means "lover," it can also carry the connotation of dabbler, dilettante, a person who is somehow preordained never to be very good. To describe someone's work as amateurish usually is not a compliment, and the expression "rank amateur" is less than inspiring. But amateur status can be joyous—denoting free choice, pure love of the doing, and open-ended possibilities for discovery.

Advantages of maturity

I teach at a university, and whenever I talk with colleagues, no matter what their subject area happens to be, we invariably agree: it's uniquely stimulating to work with the so-called nontraditional student. This is the official institutional term for the older person, the fifty-year-old in the class with all the twenty-year-olds.

Why is it stimulating? Older students have made their own choice to be there, so they want their learning to be meaningful. They are excited by the chance to master new things. They ask penetrating questions. They instigate and respond to conversations in which the teacher can also learn a lot, often making interesting connections, on a mature level, between new material or concepts and the knowledge they already have. Such connections expand everyone's understanding.

And adults can draw on their full personal histories. Professionals have arrived at a sense of mastery in a certain field and have usually become autonomous learners in the process; a lawyer or schoolteacher may say, "School was OK as far as it went, but the actual learning started when I got out in the real world." Whatever adults' experience has consisted of— work, child rearing, relationships— they've known the rich texture of life-learning. They've learned to take risks, be flexible, gain insight from their own "sovereign" mistakes, be curious, and—through all such experiences—reach a deeper level of self-acceptance. They've got some common sense and know how to focus.

> *Adults have common sense and know how to focus.*

In other words, the down-to-earth approach I recommend throughout this book fits beautifully with the profile of adult learners. Is their motor learning somewhat slower than that of a child? Certainly. But this is far outweighed by all the learning benefits just mentioned. I think that success for adult learners boils down to just one key factor: adventurousness.

Another adult cello-beginner who wrote about the experience (and who met with greater musical success than he ever expected to) was John Holt; his wise, straightforward musical memoir is titled *Never Too Late*. Interestingly, the *Los Angeles Times* called the book "delightfully subversive." Holt became famous as a courageous and visionary educational reformer, and his books about the school system (including *How Children Fail* and *How Children Learn*) became widely influential. Holt personifies the adventurous adult amateur.

Holt's musical development was strongly influenced by his own passionate ideas about education. For example, he thought that what many saw as a learning disability in schoolchildren was in fact just fear and tension, that problem readers didn't have "word blindness" as much as "fear blindness."[5] Think of how the brains of many of us become paralyzed whenever we're presented with one of those dreaded "word problems" in math—that's the feeling. Holt felt that many children were simply "too scared to learn or think." The same phrase could often be applied to the music lesson experience. Holt certainly had to battle his own fears about performing music; describing a flute solo he once attempted, he says:

> I didn't make very many mistakes, but at every one I was flooded with embarrassment and shame. I grew more and more tense, my face felt hot, my hands sweated so much I feared I would drop the flute, there was a kind of buzzing in my ears, I could hardly hear the piano. In a way, feeling great fear is like feeling great pain; it is like being inside a little box of one-way glass; others can see and hear you, but for you the world almost disappears.[6]

Holt was so innately curious about such phenomena that he was able to see them objectively and thus move beyond the trap of fear. In fact, his flute study had belonged to an earlier period of his adult life when he wasn't quite ready to blossom as he did later with the cello. He attributed his early lack of success to several factors, including, first, that he was only thinking of music as a hobby and not expecting much improvement; second, that he wasn't "psychologically or emotionally ready to play a musical instrument" because of excessive fear and shame about mistakes; third, that he wasn't physically exuberant enough in his playing; and fourth, that he wasn't resourceful enough as a practicer, but just did as he was told, even when the results were disappointing. He had yet to become an adult in the music studio or make full use of what adults are good at: taking an "intelligent, critical, and imaginative" leading role in their own processes, including musical ones. As Holt put it, "I was not yet ready to be at the center of my own learning."[7]

Chapter 10

Grown-up practicing

I learned to respect the power of grown-up practicing from "Larry," a student I taught years ago, during my graduate student days. Larry, in his mid-thirties, was a postal worker, an amiable, beefy fellow with thick fingers that could occasionally get stuck between the black keys on the piano. He had discovered that he was a songwriter, meaning that original songs kept popping into his head in full-fledged form, and he needed a way to play them. So he was seeking instrumental skills for quite a practical purpose.

He was so open, motivated, and willing to try whatever I proposed that I was really able to put my ideas to the test. Having never studied the piano before, he presented a clean slate, with no inner conflicts, no prior piano lesson traumas to unravel. Add to this his calm and stable temperament—his "maturity"—and I knew I was in luck; I sensed that the conditions were perfect for an experiment in adult learning.

So we embarked on a program of mastering the foundations of piano technique. The goals may have been a bit more ambitious than he had originally bargained for, but Larry never complained. He practiced steadily, compared himself to no one, and his expectations were relaxed. His instrumental capabilities seemed about average (although such assessments are not always fair to make). Whenever something worked he was satisfied; whenever it didn't he was patient. I threw him a lot of technical challenges but never mentioned that those skills were supposed to be hard. He was so generally pleased to be doing this that he dealt with all obstacles with honesty and equanimity as they arose. He took things apart intelligently (something adults can do well) and never took shortcuts. He combined a naturally relaxed state of mind with a rigorous approach to problem solving, and the results were solid.

. To my amazement, after about a year he was playing a Beethoven sonata with fluent, secure technique and solid musicality. People rarely play at their full capacity, but that's exactly what

208

he seemed to be doing—sometimes I secretly thought he was even playing a bit beyond his capacity! Typically, Larry treated his accomplishments with equanimity too.

Unknown to Larry, he gave me a priceless, enduring gift: a greater trust in my own instincts about learning. I suspected then, and it has since turned out to be the case, that such an untainted opportunity to find out what an adult student can do is extraordinarily rare. But accomplishments like Larry's needn't be rare; what made it work for him was simply his attitude: sane, honest, unafraid.

Adults often do have an easier time than younger students adapting to practice approaches that are thoughtful, efficient, and perhaps a bit philosophical. For example, the concept of deliberately relinquishing physical control in order to receive honest information about technique is a sophisticated one, even though it's simple to do once a person catches on to it. Adults are intrigued by such ideas. Similarly, the mental transition process into a practice-ready state is more readily understood by an adult. It appeals to adult intelligence to understand practice sessions as bold experimentation and detective work rather than dutiful repetition.

John Holt quotes the words he heard from cellist János Starker that changed his life, resonating as they did with Holt's own fervent belief in the vast educational possibilities we have as adults:

> "Well, it's extremely difficult for someone of our age to
> learn to play this instrument well, because we have to
> develop a whole new set of muscles, and a whole new set
> of coordinations." He paused an instant to let that sink in.
> "On the other hand," he said, "we have an advantage."
> "What's that?" I asked. He said, "We can think up prob-
> lems, and find solutions."[8]

Other musical pleasures

Adult amateurs who have written about their musical involve-ments often mention, and puzzle over, the tears that spring to their eyes when there is a moment of piercing beauty, when things come together and the music seems to live on its own. Whatever those tears may mean, they explain—in a way that can never be verbal-ized—the closeness of music to our very souls. In radio journalist Noah Adams's chronicle of studying music as an adult beginner entitled *Piano Lessons: Music, Love, and True Adventures*, a seasoned teacher is asked why music affects our emotions so directly, espe-cially when we're playing. She says, "Music can create these beau-tiful moments out of nothing. We can be sitting here and play a phrase and suddenly there's beauty." Having such glimpses of another realm she considers a "privilege."[9]

Often the sense of beauty seems most immediate when we make music with others, whether it's a chamber trio, a duet, a drumming circle, or a barbershop quartet. Then we have the perfect combination, in a way—we are participating actively at the same time that the shared expression transcends our own egos. The delights of this can be felt at any level of musical advancement.

In addition to instrumental study, there are other musical sat-isfactions for adults, activities that don't involve systematic practic-ing. Classes in Dalcroze Eurhythmics, for example, offer adults the same rhythmic fun and integrated learning through body move-ment that preschoolers receive. There are also grass-roots associa-tions devoted to freely expressive improvisation, requiring no train-ing or experience; the most notable of these is called Music for People. Voice and simple percussion instruments are the primary media for their improvisation sessions. Among the points in this organization's "A Bill of Musical Rights" are:

- Musical self-expression is a joyful and healthy means of communication available to absolutely everyone.

- There are as many different ways to make music as there are people.
- In improvisation as in life, we must be responsible for the vibrations we send one another.[10]

Researchers are just beginning to investigate the health benefits of music participation, but the findings seem convincing and heartening. A recent study analyzed the saliva of volunteer members of a community chorale in California, measuring the amounts of certain antibodies made up of disease-fighting proteins. They were tested before, during, and after rehearsals, and at a performance. Not only did the level of immunoglobin A rise 150 percent after the rehearsals; it spiked 240 percent after the performance. This surprised the researchers, who had theorized that the performance might be stressful and thus lower the level. But apparently performing proved to be a peak experience of a positive kind. They also concluded from the data that the more passionately the choristers sang, the more their antibody level rose.[11]

Primarily, though, it is the personal stories that impress. Michigan State music professor Midori Koga writes of her grandfather in Tokyo picking up the violin again at the age of eighty and performing his first solo recital at his own eighty-eighth birthday celebration. He found a good teacher, practiced diligently, played some chamber music which inspired him even more, and awoke each day in his eighties "happy to know that I have so much to learn today." According to Koga, he "played as a child plays, wholeheartedly, joyfully and with pure abandon."[12]

Clearly, adults need to choose a teacher thoughtfully. Amateurs who have written about their musical journeys have been candid about the destructiveness of some teachers and the skillful helpfulness of others. Pre-lesson interviews are essential. Good teachers for adults understand the paralyzing dangers of misplaced perfectionism, and know how to encourage grown-up problem-solving autonomy. Again I defer to the firsthand account of adventurous amateur John Holt:

> The teacher I need must accept that he or she is my partner and helper and not my boss, that in this journey of musical exploration and adventure, I am the captain. Expert guides and pilots I can use, no doubt about it. But it is my expedition; I gain the most if it succeeds and lose the most if it fails, and I must remain in charge.[13]

11 | Beyond the Music Room

Music participation should be healthy, both mentally and physically, because only then can we reap its precious harvest. What are the most important fruits of that harvest?

LIBERATION—from the distorting grip of ego, from shame and fear, from the futility of trying to control every outcome

SERENITY—benevolent acceptance of how things are, and trust in the possibility of transformation

VITALITY—energized body and mind, spontaneous emotions, a tangible sense of connection with others, bold risk-taking

HONESTY—participation in a process that exposes self-deception

HUMILITY—letting go of false pride; learning equally from every result, successful or not

AWARENESS—of small details, large gestalts, and how reality shifts from moment to moment

BEAUTY—of being open to the penetrating power of music, of discovering new meaning through giving something away (sharing that beauty with others in performance).

As you look over this list, try removing all specific references to music. What's left? Human values of substance and depth: liberation, serenity, vitality, honesty, humility, awareness, and beauty.

If a person making music receives only a portion of such gifts, the adventure has been undoubtedly worthwhile.

This brings us to another way of thinking about the quest of mastering music performance, a way to view it from the other end of the telescope, so to speak. Not only should we ask how we can serve music well, but also how our musical strivings serve us. My answer is this: qualities to which we aspire in our lives in general, but sometimes find rather abstract and elusive, are made concrete by musical processes. Music study presents a natural, here-and-now route to self-knowledge and self-integration; in this light, some might even call it a spiritual practice, and a handy, effortless one too, since we're usually not thinking about profound issues while practicing; we're just trying to get the music right. The key is that we're going about it with an awakened sense of awareness, free of irrelevant fantasies or fears.

Having a job to do can cleanse and open the mind; when Zen masters are asked about the path to enlightenment, they usually answer "sweep the floor" or "wash the dishes," the idea being to perform these down-to-earth tasks with total, selfless, appreciative mindfulness. Musical work at its most practical level can be effective in just that way.

For example, a student tells me that he struggles daily with a tendency to be too "prideful," but for the hour he's practicing music he knows that all pridefulness has vanished, solely because of how the practice process works, and without any special effort on his part. That hour brings out his best self, and he senses it. Similarly, while many of us may find philosophical phrases like "be present in the moment" or "let go of your attachments" maddeningly elusive at times, musical experiences capture their meaning clearly. Paradoxes suddenly make sense when we're practicing music; ancient philosophies such as "If you would become strong, first be weak" or "In order to gain control, relinquish control" find a living model in the hands-on arena of musical technique.

The dissolving of ego-consciousness in general, so crucial in practicing and performing, is indeed a universal value; according to Aldous Huxley, for most people "the urge to escape, the longing to transcend themselves if only for a few moments, is and always has been a principal appetite of the soul."[1] We do seem to have that appetite, and we find countless ways to forget ourselves for a time— entertainment, mind-altering substances, sports and games, sensual pleasures, food, hard work, nature walks, meditation, prayer, the absorption of listening to or making music. But there are some uniquely rich nuances to the musical experience.

Writer and literary critic Eva Hoffman was a trained pianist of talent who at one time considered a musical career. Thanks to a wise and special piano teacher in her native Poland, Hoffman as a teenager became aware through music of "the motions and conduct of my inner life" and sensed that she was receiving a kind of "moral education." She awoke to the fact that music was more than pretty sounds but an eloquent "language of emotions," especially regarding something quite specific: the tone quality one produces at the piano.

> Tone, I discover, is something about which I cannot lie. If I
> do not feel the kindling of a fire as I play, my tone betrays
> me by its coldness; if I do not feel the capricious light-
> heartedness of a scherzo, my tone turns wooden in spite of
> my best attempts to feign playfulness. By some inexplicable
> process, the precise nuance of what I feel is conveyed
> through my arm to my fingertips, and then, through those
> fingertips, to the piano keys.[2]

This connection with the piano, or any instrument, is in fact a two-way communication, in which the player receives information too. In Hoffman's words, "If the spirit is to flow into the keys through the conduit of my arm and hand, it has to move in the other direction as well—from the keys into my arm and soul." Her teacher keeps reminding her to "let the music be itself." "It is to this end that one has to relax, relax as much as possible—relax one's arm and one's self, so that one can become the medium through which the music flows as naturally as melting snow in the spring." But relaxation isn't everything, Hoffman rightly adds, since we also need strong, reliable technique to free us from distracting worries about whether we'll be able to manage the next tricky passage or risky jump. Technique is worth building because, as Hoffman puts it, "Music may express the deepest truths, but it expresses them through a material medium," and this happens best when the physical materials are mastered.

Alchemy

The ancient, mystical art of alchemy, the occult science of transforming lead into gold, was something we scoffed at in our high-school chemistry class. How ignorant they were in the old days, we thought. But the idea behind alchemy is timeless and relevant.

The medieval images associated with alchemy are symbolic and bizarre: a green lion eating the sun, a snake swallowing its own tail, a black sun, and so on. Ordinary objects became surreal, existing in a dream-world or parallel reality. But are such images really so strange? Everyday consciousness can change momentarily into a more transcendent mental state, a flash of insight during which everything looks different. This is something we all glimpse briefly in life. The power of alchemy is as a metaphor for such transformation. As Morris Berman has written, "The gold of which [the alchemists] spoke was thus not really gold, but a 'golden' state of mind, the altered state of consciousness which overwhelms the person in an experience such as the Zen satori or the God-experience recorded by Western mystics."[3]

What's useful here is not only what alchemy was, but how it worked. It seems to have involved a radical breaking down, a dissolving, of the "normal" substance at hand. The Latin formula most often used by alchemists was *solve et coagula*, which simply means that the original substance must first dissolve in order to coagulate later into the new "gold."

It is not so easy to let the familiar world dissolve. But this is how we can open the door to transformation. At a particular juncture in my own work, several thought-provoking encounters with others jarred my complacency and seriously rattled my basic understandings of teaching and playing. All my ground rules seemed to have gone out the window. But to my surprise this felt energizing, not scary; apparently the jarring came at the right moment. I sensed that I wasn't discarding prior beliefs wholesale or endorsing some rigid duality that ordained new ideas to be right and older ones wrong. I simply was no longer clinging to the familiar. All bets were off, and I trusted that the best ideas would emerge naturally from the transformation process, because I was letting my attachment to certain beliefs dissolve.

In general terms, conventional patterns must dissolve into chaos—or what appears to be chaos—in order to find the gold of alchemy: truer knowledge. Music gives us opportunity after opportunity to discover this. Performers must let the persona, the individual social shell, dissolve into the expressive stream of the music itself in order to deliver a convincing, vital performance. And in the practice-room, the clever right notes—achieved by willpower and the self-conscious efforts of muscles and nerves—must dissolve into the "chaos" of physical freedom (and momentary wrong notes) in order to recoagulate as integrated, "golden" technical control. When such a release happens, a musician can experience transformation—from a student into a virtuoso.

The procedures of alchemy were not rigidly prescribed and were thus not taught in detail. Tradition held that each student had to figure them out for himself. Each situation was unique. But the basic philosophy *was* definitely taught: that *solve et coagula* could lead to transformation.[4] Alchemy thus provides us with a model, a helpful way to think about music lessons, art lessons, acting lessons—perhaps lessons in anything.

A new kind of information

Albert Einstein made the oft-quoted statement that in an age of nuclear bombs everything had changed except the way we thought, and humankind would need a "new manner of thinking" in order to survive in the years to come. He didn't explain exactly what this meant, which has certainly been a frustration to those who looked to him for answers, As intensely as Einstein agonized about the implications of the bomb's existence, it seems unlikely to me that he would have withheld an explanation on purpose; but I believe that his insight was probably something that words couldn't capture. We know from his violin playing that Einstein himself solved difficult problems using physical findings (about patterns and relationships, perhaps) that could never be explained in words.

Other scientists have also looked to music as a special problem-solving medium and as a means of understanding and representing abstract concepts. Michael Polanyi (1891–1976) was a world-renowned chemist who turned to philosophy in later life and achieved great prominence as a thinker. Polanyi went beyond the objective scientific method in which he was trained when he said that humans "know more than we can tell": there are important truths which are personal and irreducible and which can never be analyzed or described. This view acknowledges that the scientific method will not always be adequate, since science takes a reductionist approach—one that reduces a big question to smaller, more manageable ones without necessarily ever answering the big question.

To illustrate the shortcomings of reductionist analysis, Polanyi turned to piano technique as an example. In fact, this passage reveals far more insight into piano playing than many books by musicians do! Polanyi understood that since the body will always be more sophisticated than the mind, its workings at a certain level can never be explained by one person to another.

> The analysis of a skillful feat in terms of its constituent motions remains always incomplete. There are notorious cases, like the distinctive "touch" of a pianist, in which the analysis of a skill has long been debated inconclusively; and common experience shows that no skill can be acquired by learning its constituent motions separately. Moreover, here too isolation modifies the particulars: their dynamic quality is lost. Indeed, the identification of the constituent motions of a skill tends to paralyse its performance. Only by turning our attention away from the particulars and towards their joint purpose, can we restore to the isolated motions the qualities required for achieving their purpose. . . . This act of integration is itself unspecifiable. Imitation offers guidance to it, but in the last resort we must rely on discovering for ourselves the right feel of a skillful feat. We alone can catch the knack of it; no teacher can do this for us.[5]

Polanyi has captured the essence of making music: good, purposeful practice results in a dynamic and irreducible "act of integration." Integration of a person through music can take many forms; sometimes these manifestations can be quite uncanny. In neurologist Oliver Sacks's book of "clinical tales" called *The Man Who Mistook His Wife for a Hat*, music is a recurring theme. Many of

> *Integration of a person through music can take many forms.*

Sacks's true stories concern people with damaged brains and neurological deficits whose only intact mental functioning pertained to music, such as the woman with drastic memory loss who had no trouble remembering every word to a popular song she used to sing decades before. Sacks observed that the expressive element of "music, narrative and drama" seemed to organize the minds and functioning of the patients he worked with; for example, a man with a severe stutter loved to perform in musicals, since whenever he was performing a song in character his stutter disappeared completely. People whose mental challenges made it difficult to retain a simple sequence of four or five tasks to perform, could succeed "perfectly if they work to music—the sequence of movements they cannot hold as schemes being perfectly holdable as music, i.e. imbedded in music."[6] Sacks's book celebrates "the power of music to organise—and to do this efficaciously (as well as joyfully!), when abstract or schematic forms of organization fail."[7]

Another contemporary research scientist of prominence—and of adventurous integrative thought—is Candace Pert. By meticulously tracking and measuring what she calls "biochemicals of emotion," Pert is providing new evidence of our mind-body-spirit interrelatedness. In views such as hers, the human being is a sophisticated open-system complex of information exchange—physical, chemical, electrical—that operates through constant feedback. The more attuned we are to such feedback within us, the healthier we are. As we saw in chapter 3, music practice is an ideal opportunity for subtle internal feedback loops, for heightening that honest self-awareness. And in good practicing, we approach inner feedback with the same interested impartiality that scientific investigators bring to their findings. Information science is the stimulating new frontier for researchers like Pert:

> Information! It is the missing piece that allows us to transcend the mind-body split of the Cartesian view, because by definition, information belongs to neither mind nor body, although it touches both. We must accept that it occupies a whole new realm, one we can perhaps call the "inforealm," which science has yet to explore. Information

theory releases us from the trap of reductionism and its tenets of positivism, determinism, and objectivism. Although these basic assumptions of Western science have been ingrained in our consciousness since the sixteenth and seventeenth centuries, information theory constitutes such a new language—a rich language of relatedness, cooperation, interdependence, and synergy rather than simple force and response—that it helps us break out of our old patterns of thought.[8]

Again and again we see that to be open to helpful new information requires a release of some sort—releasing old thoughts, or rigid ego-focus, or unhealthy reliance on a teacher, or certain muscles in the arm. And after we have released, we simply observe, with keen investigatory interest, and respond to the new information. Of course this isn't always so easy to do. When there are deadlines, like having to be ready on a certain date to perform a piece of music in public, it can be very difficult to release and much more tempting to cling to past results. This is where trust comes in—trust in ourselves and in the wisdom of healthy processes. Releasing and trusting remind me of certain Eastern philosophies which have been introduced to the West as "Zen" formulas for success, for meeting goals in business or any other field of endeavor. They advise us to form a sincere intention, release it into the universe with trust and the acknowledgment that everything can't be controlled, and then pay ego-less attention to whatever results ensue. What better way to get used to doing this than to process our way through some wrong musical notes on the pathway to the right ones?

Philosophical and spiritual writers often turn to music as a way to crystallize human experience. Aldous Huxley, in his essay "Man and Religion," equates the process of music mastery with another vital, selfless activity: prayer.

This attitude of the masters of prayer is in its final analysis exactly the same as that recommended by the teacher of any psychophysical skill. The man who teaches you how to play golf or tennis, your singing teacher or piano teacher, will tell you the same thing: you must somehow combine activity with relaxation, you must let go of the clutching personal self, in order to let this deeper self within you, which you interfere with, come through and perform its miracles.[9]

As we celebrate such miracles and the interconnectedness of music to other parts of our being, let us not forget what will always make this human activity so unique: the ineffable humanity of beautiful music itself. Sublime music is greater than any individual person, even greater (some would say) than the composer who received the inspiration to write it down in the first place. It has implications that bring mysterious tears to our eyes, it stirs and delights us, it gives us fresh understandings of our own inner life of thought and feeling and our connection with others.

Music, the most abstract and uncanny art, is an eternal river of sound moving through time. We can free ourselves from whatever may be holding us back, and join that flowing river.

Postscript
A Word to Health Professionals

Conservatories and symphony orchestras, as many are aware, are rife with hurting and injured musicians. To realize that music-making itself has caused painful, chronic bodily harm is devastating, depressing, and scary for anyone who has been devoted to the musical art and who has invested in it professionally and worked for years at mastering its craft. On top of that, such injuries can precipitate a major identity crisis (if I was born to be a musician, how could this be happening?).

Clearly, music teachers aren't qualified to diagnose and treat serious physical ailments; a medical professional must be sought. Thus the new specialty of arts medicine has come into being, and its practitioners have benefited musicians greatly, making us more aware of ways to stay healthy while working hard at music—such as taking frequent breaks and noticing body alignment. We've also come to understand that having good general health going into a practice session is crucial and that we can actively promote our musical health through good diet, exercise, and stretching. But when a problem does arise, ways of dealing with it can still be a bit murky; theories about the causes of performance-related injury remain controversial, and treatment protocols vary widely and are not always effective.

The implication seems clear: preventing injury is by far the best policy. Yet if an injury does occur, a different sort of opportunity presents itself: to gain good insight from it in order to prevent a recurrence. In that way the whole episode can be valuable and positive in the long run, which I have seen happen many times with students.

Musical injuries are not usually caused by diseases or freak accidents; they are usually caused over time by something we are habitually doing. And if a doctor treats only the symptoms without figuring out what the musician did to cause them, that injury will most likely redevelop (with even more devastating impact). Here's where things get a bit dicey: how can a doctor or physical therapist feel qualified to advise an impressive, advanced musician on how to practice "right"?

Let's look at a typical scenario. The brilliant, prize-winning Juilliard piano student comes to the doctor complaining of arm pain. The doctor, an amateur violinist and avid music-lover who has only played music of intermediate difficulty and never as a soloist in public, is genuinely in awe of any brilliantly talented musician. So the doctor doesn't question the pianist about her philosophy of practicing, but instead limits himself to generic advice about posture, alignment, ease, rest, warm-ups, frequent breaks in practice, and so on. The student does better for a while, but as the recital date looms her practicing intensifies, the problem recurs, and the recital has to be canceled because of the injury.

What has caused the problem? Is it possible that this truly gifted pianist is not using basic common sense in the practice room? Could she in fact be harming herself by working in a subtly self-destructive way that really needs to be rethought? Could certain conflicts be so hidden that no one has been aware of them?

Conflicts and unrealistic thinking can indeed create physical difficulties in daily practice. To interrupt the cycle and bring about real improvement, we need to keep certain basic precepts in mind:

- The body and mind are integrated in their functioning.
- Body-mind conflicts express themselves through subtle physical tension, which can accumulate over time and lead to injury.

- To get well and stay well, we must identify and remove inner conflicts.
- To do so requires common sense and not any specific musical or psychological expertise.

Conflict, in anatomical terms, can be understood like this: I have only one right arm. I'd like to use it only for playing the phrases, with natural flow, enjoyment, and connection to the rhythm of my whole body. If I use my right arm instead to supervise itself, to guarantee the accuracy and aesthetic perfection of each note (no matter how slowly I may do so), it's not the same feeling at all. That's why it's imperative that I learn how to "relinquish control" whenever I choose to. One arm shouldn't try to do two contradictory acts at once, namely placing each note carefully and playing it freely. Either I'm clutching or I'm letting go; I can't do both at the same time. If I try to, I have a body-mind conflict, and invite injury.

If this is indeed the fundamental conflict (as it frequently is with high achievers), in addition to giving the customary sound advice about healthy posture and physical ease, the doctor can probe for the underlying cause of tension and injury. To shed light on the cause does not require any knowledge of music on the doctor's part, but rather just knowing what questions to ask and how to pay attention to the answers. Any doctor who has read this book and is in tune with its central thesis will know immediately how to respond constructively to the patient's answers. Here are the types of questions one can ask of a musician in pain:

1. Do you allow imperfections in the practice room, or do you suppress them? Describe your thought process when something goes wrong. Do you take it personally, feel guilty? Are you patient and creative about finding solutions to problems? Do you embrace and enjoy that problem-solving process?

2. What information do you get from your body while you practice? (If the patient answers "none," there is clearly a problem. A more desirable answer would be something like, "I always assess whether my actions are comfortable or not.")

3. Do you strive to play artistically all the time, even in practice? (The answer you are looking for: "Of course not!")

4. Do you believe that your teacher expects you to play everything with polish and accuracy at every lesson? What would happen if you didn't, if you weren't quite ready to show finished results on a given day? Would you be letting that teacher down, or feel that you are humiliating yourself? (If the answer here is basically "yes," you must proceed with tact and caution: allegiance to teachers can be very strong and it's not always useful to contradict them directly. But students do need to hear a realistic viewpoint from someone, and you may well be the only person in a position to offer it.)

5. How do you define a successful practice session? (Notice how the answer is phrased, whether in terms of perfectionistic results or actual quality of experience.)

As I have pointed out many times in this book, good practicing consists of a continuous stream of moment-to-moment decisions, none of them predictable. An underlying philosophy needs to govern those decisions. It's beneficial for all musicians to bring that philosophy into consciousness, and it helps greatly to talk it out thoughtfully with someone. That someone needn't be the music teacher and can just as well be a health professional.

A competitive atmosphere can cloud performers' thinking. Pressures on advanced musicians are great, and students at all levels tend to be self-critical, excruciatingly aware of the brilliance of their rivals and of the (manufactured) perfection of the recordings they hear. Classical music training in many quarters also has had that long tradition of requiring students to win their teachers' approval in every lesson, with errors not tolerated. Add to this family pressures to be the best, or a self-image heavily invested in musical excellence, and the possibility of distorted thinking becomes considerable.

Thus it's easy for one's point of view to get turned around backward—to take the practice process for granted and to question oneself, instead of accepting oneself and questioning the basic approach to practicing.

If I were a medical practitioner, I'd say to a worried and hurting musician something like this: As you practice, sense that you're taking good care of yourself at every moment. Expect musical performing to be fun and feel good. Question any part of it that doesn't feel that way. Think of yourself as a healthy athlete. Relax frequently and take stock. Use lots of body energy to vitalize and support your actions at the instrument. Don't pretend you can control everything at every moment; mastery comes to you over time when you're focused. Don't get ahead of yourself. Always be patient and curious about imperfections. Remember the simple formula about harmful tension: zero plus zero, when added together an infinite number of times, will still total zero. And when the level of harmful tension is zero, injuries cannot happen to you.

Resources

The organizations and resources listed here are dedicated to helping people awaken their musical instincts and skills. All welcome participants at various musical levels.

Amateur Chamber Music Players
1123 Broadway, Room 304
New York, New York 10010-2007
Phone: 212 645-7424
Fax: 212 741-2678
Email: webmaster@acmp.net

International network of amateur musicians at various levels of experience and ability.

Dalcroze Society of America
2812 Fairmount Boulevard
Cleveland Heights, Ohio 44118-4020
http://www.dalcrozeusa.org

Courses in various locations, including summer sessions, open to all. From the society's Web site: "Dalcroze training stimulates, develops, and refines all the capacities we use when we engage in music: our senses of hearing, sight, and touch; our faculties of knowing and reasoning; our ability to feel and to act on our feelings. Coordinating these capacities is the kinesthetic sense, the feedback mechanism of the nervous system which conveys information between the mind and the body. The education of this sense to the purposes of music is at the heart of the Dalcroze work."

Music for People
187 Sherbrook Drive, Box 397
Goshen, Connecticut 06756
Phone: 860 491-3763 or toll-free 877 446-8742
Fax: 860 491-4513
http://www.musicforpeople.org

Improvisation sessions in informal settings, plus longer workshops throughout the year.

Music Teachers National Association
441 Vine Street, Suite 505
Cincinnati, Ohio 45202-2811
Phone: 888 512-5278 or 513 421-1420
Fax: 513 421-2503
Email: mtnanet@mtna.org
http://www.mtna.org

Assistance locating certified studio teachers.

William Westney
School of Music
Texas Tech University
Lubbock, Texas 79409-2033
http://www.williamwestney.com

Lectures, workshops, performances, consultations, and residencies.

Notes

Chapter 1
1. Heinlein 1991, 265–266.
2. Samples 1976, 93.
3. Coulter 1989.
4. Brown 1988, 232.
5. Huizinga 1980, 10.
6. De Mille 1981, 130.
7. Langer 1951, 110.
8. Hampden-Turner 1981, 100.
9. Cobb 1959.
10. Ferguson 1980, 284.
11. Lao Tzu 1944, 48.
12. Gardner 1982, 89.
13. Krishnamurti 1982, 45.
14. Langer 1951, ix.

Chapter 2
1. "Prisons" 1992, 18.
2. Fay 1880, 82.
3. Fay 1880, 212.
4. Matthay 1913, 3.
5. Rogers 1961, 276.
6. Matthay 1913, 20.
7. Sand 2000, 67.
8. Gardner 1982, 200.
9. Ristad 1982, 53.
10. Fay 1880, 123.
11. Hagen 1997, 21.

Chapter 3
1. Newman 1984, 125–127.
2. Foldes 1948, 48.
3. Gieseking and Leimer 1932, 47.
4. Raban 1991, 286.
5. Briggs and Pear 1989, 21.
6. Schaef 1987, 69.
7. Briggs and Pear 1989, 165–177.
8. Chase 1966, 4.

Chapter 4
1. Perls 1969, 51.
2. McCluggage 1983, 69.

Chapter 5
1. Edwards 1979, 106–107.
2. Feynman 1986, 311.
3. Guinness 1985, 158.
4. Kamen 1984.

Chapter 6
1. Feynman 1985, 36.
2. Perls 1969, 18.

Chapter 7
1. Whone 1974, 91.

Chapter 8
1. See, for example, Hampden-Turner 1981, 102.
2. Hofstadter 1979, 611.
3. Hofstadter 1979, 612.
4. Ristad 1982, 164.
5. Edwards 1999, 57.
6. Nachmanovitch 1990, 52.

Chapter 9
1. The Un-Master Class® is a registered service mark, and rights
   to its use are reserved; please see copyright page.
2. Holland 1999.

Chapter 10
1. Doyle 1930, 11.
2. Clark 1971, 106.
3. Rehak 1999.
4. Booth 1999, 73.
5. Holt 1978, 132.
6. Holt 1978, 128.
7. Holt 1978, 135.
8. Holt 1978, 179.
9. Adams 1996, 220.
10. Music for People 2001.
11. Fisher 2001.
12. Koga 2001.
13. Holt 1978, 217.

Chapter 11
1. Huxley 1954, 62.
2. Hoffman 1989, 70.
3. Berman 1981, 73.
4. Berman, 1981, 79.
5. Polanyi 1969, 126.
6. Sacks 1985, 185.
7. Sacks 1985, 186.
8. Pert 1997, 261.
9. Huxley 1977, 214.

Bibliography

Adams, Noah. 1996. *Piano Lessons: Music, Love, and True Adventures.*
New York: Random House.

Berman, Morris. 1981. *The Reenchantment of the World.* New York:
Cornell University Press.

Booth, Wayne. 1999. *For the Love of It.* Chicago: University of Chicago
Press.

Briggs, John, and David F. Pear. 1989. *Turbulent Mirror: An Illustrated
Guide to Chaos Theory and the Science of Wholeness.* New York:
Harper & Row.

Brown, Kenneth A. 1988. *Inventors at Work.* Redmond, Washington:
Tempus Books of Microsoft Press.

Chase, Stuart. 1966. *The Tyranny of Words.* San Diego: Harvest HBJ.

Clark, Ronald W. 1971. *Einstein: The Life and Times.* New York: World
Publishing Co.

Cobb, Edith. 1959. "The Ecology of Imagination in Childhood." *Daedalus*
88 (3).

Coulter, Dee. 1989. *The Inner-Dynamics of Creativity.* Boulder, Colorado:
Sounds True Recordings. Audiotape.

De Mille, Agnes. 1981. *Reprieve: A Memoir.* Garden City, New York:
Doubleday.

Doyle, Sir Arthur Conan. 1930. "A Study in Scarlet" in *The Complete
Sherlock Holmes.* Garden City, New York: Doubleday.

Edwards, Betty. 1979. *Drawing on the Right Side of the Brain.* Los Angeles:
J. P. Tarcher.

Edwards, Betty. 1999. *The New Drawing on the Right Side of the Brain.*
New York: Tarcher/Putnam.

Fay, Amy. 1880. *Music-Study in Germany.* Chicago: A. C. McClurg & Co.

Ferguson, Marilyn. 1980. *The Aquarian Conspiracy.* Los Angeles: J. P.
Tarcher.

Feynman, Richard. 1985. *Surely You're Joking, Mr. Feinman!* New York: W.
W. Norton.

Bibliography

Fisher, Marla Jo. 2001. "Study Finds that Choral Singing Boosts Production of Antibodies that Fight Disease." *The Voice of Chorus America Newsletter* (Summer). http://www.chorusamerica.org/voice_article_health.shtml

Foldes, Andor. 1948. *Keys to the Keyboard*. New York: E. P. Dutton.

Gallwey, W. Timothy. 1974. *The Inner Game of Tennis*. New York: Random House.

Gardner, Howard. 1982. *Art, Mind and Brain*. New York: Basic Books.

Gieseking, Walter, and Karl Leimer. 1932. *Piano Technique: The Shortest Way to Pianistic Perfection*. London: Schott.

Guinness, Alec. 1985. *Blessings in Disguise*. New York: Warner Books.

Hagen, Steve. 1997. *Buddhism Plain and Simple*. New York: Broadway Books.

Hampden-Turner, Charles. 1981. *Maps of the Mind*. New York: Collier Books.

Heinlein, Robert A. 1991. *Stranger in a Strange Land*. New York: Putnam.

Hoffman, Eva. 1989. *Lost in Translation*. New York: E. P. Dutton.

Hofstadter, Douglas. 1979. *Gödel, Escher, Bach: An Eternal Golden Braid*. New York: Basic Books.

Holland, Bernard. 1999. "Star Turns by Star Teachers: Classes in the Callas Tradition." *The New York Times* (January 27).

Holt, John. 1978. *Never Too Late*. New York: Delacorte Press.

Houston, Jean. 1982. *The Possible Human*. Los Angeles: J. P. Tarcher.

Huizinga, Johan. 1980. *Homo Ludens: A Study of the Play-Element in Culture*. London: Routledge & K. Paul.

Huxley, Aldous. 1954. *The Doors of Perception*. New York: Harper & Row.

Huxley, Aldous. 1977. *The Human Situation*. New York: Harper & Row.

Kamen, Robert Mark. 1984. *The Karate Kid*. Burbank, California: Columbia Tristar Home Video. Videorecording.

Koga, Midori, and Frederick Tims. 2001. "The Music Making and Wellness Project." *American Music Teacher* (October/November).

Krishnamurti, J. 1982. *The Network of Thought*. San Francisco: Harper & Row.

Langer, Susanne K. 1951. *Philosophy in a New Key*. Cambridge, Massachusetts: Harvard University Press.

Lao Tzu. 1944. *The Way of Life*. Trans. Witter Bynner. New York: Putnam.

Matthay, Tobias. 1913. *Musical Interpretation, Its Laws and Principles, and Their Application in Teaching and Performing.* Boston: The Boston Music Co.

McCluggage, Denise. 1983. *The Centered Skier.* New York: Bantam Books.

Music for People. 2001. "A Bill of Musical Rights." http://www.musicfor people.org/connect/rights.html. Accessed 10 October 2002.

Nachmanovitch, Stephen. 1990. *Free Play: Improvisation in Life and Art.* Los Angeles: Jeremy P. Tarcher.

Newman, William S. 1984. *The Pianist's Problems.* New York: Da Capo Press.

Perls, Frederick S. 1969. *Gestalt Therapy Verbatim.* Moab, Utah: Real People Press.

Pert, Candace B. 1997. *Molecules of Emotion.* New York: Scribner.

Polanyi, Michael 1969. *Knowing and Being.* Chicago: University of Chicago Press.

"Prisons." 1992. *The Sun* (February).

Raban, Jonathan. 1991. *Hunting Mister Heartbreak.* New York: Harper Collins.

Rehak, Melanie. 1999. "A Joyful Noise: How to Practice Without Hope of Perfection." *The New York Times Magazine* (April 11).

Ristad, Eloise. 1982. *A Soprano on Her Head.* Moab, Utah: Real People Press.

Rogers, Carl. 1961. *On Becoming a Person.* Boston: Houghton Mifflin.

Sacks, Oliver. 1985. *The Man Who Mistook His Wife for a Hat and Other Clinical Tales.* New York: Summit Books.

Samples, Bob. 1976. *The Metaphoric Mind: A Celebration of Creative Consciousness.* Reading, Massachusetts: Addison-Wesley.

Sand, Barbara Lourie. 2000. *Teaching Genius: Dorothy DeLay and the Making of a Musician.* Portland, Oregon: Amadeus Press.

Schaef, Anne Wilson. 1987. *When Society Becomes an Addict.* New York: Harper & Row.

Spock, Benjamin. 1945. *The Common Sense Book of Baby and Child Care.* New York: Duell, Sloan and Pearce.

Whone, Herbert. 1974. *The Hidden Face of Music.* London: Gollancz.

Index

Adams, Noah, 210
adjudication, 29, 34–35
adolescents, 30–32, 67, 130–131
alchemy, 216–218
Aristotle, 66
arpeggios, 102–104
artistry, 17, 112, 115–116, 149,
    168–169, 186–187
atonality, 163–165

Bach, J. S.: French Suite No. 3 in B
    minor, 114; Prelude in G minor,
    185–187
"The Biology of Music Making,"
    32–33
brainstorming, 129, 165–167, 184
Buddhism, 49, 75

Call and Response, 192
Casals, Pablo, 85
chaos theory, 71–73, 104
Chopin, Frédéric: Nocturne in E-flat
    major, op. 9, no. 2, 109–111;
    Prelude in F-sharp major, op. 28,
    no. 13, 161
choral singing, 211
codependence, 44–45
continuum of awareness, 77–78
control, illusion of, 49, 76, 82, 113
Coulter, Dee, 20

Dalcroze Eurhythmics, 15–16, 21,
    43, 174, 188, 210
DeLay, Dorothy, 41–42
divide and conquer, 86, 154
Duncan, Isadora, 75

Edwards, Betty, 108–109, 157–158

Einstein, Albert, 20–21, 24, 104,
    201–202, 218
Evans, Edith, 112–114

Fay, Amy, 38–40, 47–48
"feelmage," 88–90
Feynman, Richard, 111, 118–119
fight or flight, 139, 141–142
Foldes, Andor, 59
fourth finger, 106–107

Gardner, Howard, 26, 43
Gestalt psychology, 77–78, 131
Gieseking, Walter, 60
golf, 204
"grokking," 19, 26
Guinness, Alec, 112–114, 119

Heinlein, Robert, 19
Hoffman, Eva, 215–216
Hofstadter, Douglas, 154–156
Holmes, Sherlock, 201
Holt, John, 206–207, 209, 212
Huxley, Aldous, 215, 221–222

improvisation, 121, 159–160,
    210–211
information science, 220–221
"inner gesture," 21
inventors, 21

Jaques-Dalcroze, Émile. *See* Dalcroze
    Eurhythmics

The Karate Kid, 115–116, 119
Kleiman, Ivan, 55–57
Koestler, Arthur, 24

236

About the Author

William Westney holds two endowed faculty positions at Texas Tech University: Paul Whitfield Horn Distinguished Professor and Browning Artist-in-Residence. He has been honored with many professional awards as educator and artist, including the Yale School of Music Alumni Association's prestigious Certificate of Merit, for his distinctive and innovative contributions to the teaching of musical performance. Westney's acclaimed Un-Master Class® performance workshop, which has been featured in The New York Times, is increasingly in demand in the United States and abroad. An active concert pianist, he has won the Geneva International Competition and holds master's and doctorate degrees in performance from Yale University.